# FIRE

## IN THE HEART

REFLECTIONS

by

FATHER FRAN ESCHWEILER

HI-TIME PUBLISHING CORP.

**Cover Design** — Sister Alice Ann Pfeifer, C.S.A.

**Copyright** © HI-TIME Publishing Corp. 1992

**HI-TIME Publishing Corp.**
Box 13337
Milwaukee, WI 53213-0337

**ISBN 0-937997-24-2**

These pages are humbly dedicated
to the HOLY SPIRIT
and to those many Spirit-filled people along the way
who have shaped my life
and "nudged" me to scribble down
what has become this little book.

# Contents

# Foreword

Who is Father Fran Eschweiler? Here at HI-TIME Publishing, we started wondering who he was immediately after we had read a manuscript of his unpublished essays. That the manuscript even exists is a testimony to the power of a small group. Father Fran began writing his thoughts at the urging of an informal discussion group with whom he regularly meets. Over a hearty breakfast, members discuss the latest books they have read and the current theological and social issues that are on their minds.

It was this discussion group that came forward with Father Fran's manuscript and asked us to consider publishing it. Soon we found ourselves sharing in their enthusiasm for the clear vision of the man who wrote it and for the years of accumulated wisdom that it expresses.

Father Fran is a retired priest whose compelling homilies attracted scores of new members to the parish he founded in the late '50s. Some forty years later, he remains active in the Archdiocese of Milwaukee. In his eight years of retirement, he has been involved in the Campaign for Human Development and in the Diocesan Ecumenical Office. When he isn't presiding at a Mass in a parish near his place of residence, he just might be preparing a talk on ecumenism, on the Church's option for the poor, or on some other topic that people readily associate with his name. Father Fran is an avid reader and letter writer, and he maintains ties with a diversity of people — some whom he knew forty years ago when he taught at the seminary and some like author Joe Nolan, whom he affectionately calls "my mentor." (Father Nolan is about twenty years younger than Father Fran!)

In the process of preparing this book, we learned that over the years many people have asked the question, "Who is Father Fran Eschweiler?" Some asked the question back in the '40s when he became involved with the labor movement. Others asked it in the '60s when he made strong public statements about open housing, birth control, and other burning issues of the day. And in the '70s author Paul Wilkes asked it while doing research for his book *These Priests Stay.* At the time, Father Fran was pastor of an active, progressive parish in a Milwaukee suburb, and Mr. Wilkes was at the beginning of a distinguished career in writing and documentary film making. (One of Mr. Wilkes' most recent projects was a two-part profile of Archbishop Rembert Weakland that appeared in *The New Yorker.*)

With the gracious consent of Mr. Wilkes, we are able to include in this book a reprint of the chapter on Father Fran from the 1973 book, *These Priests Stay.* Although this interview was written nearly twenty years ago, it still offers an accurate and vivid description of someone we have grown to admire — a free spirit ("Is it better to be an unfree spirit?" Father Fran wryly asks), an Easter person, truly a man with a fire in his heart.

THE EDITORS
June 30, 1992

# Father Francis Eschweiler
by Paul Wilkes

EDITOR'S NOTE: The following is a chapter from the book *These Priests Stay* by Paul Wilkes. New York: Simon and Schuster, 1973. Reprinted with permission of the author.

*During one week in 1909 diphtheria struck down three of the Eschweiler children. A fourth wavered, the baby Francis. Then he slowly began to recover and in the midst of grief there were prayers of thanksgiving that he had been delivered. Francis grew to be a spindly child who easily tired in the childhood games that were played in the cornfields near his home in a working-class area on Milwaukee's northwest side.*

*The Eschweilers were a family prone to going to Mass and frequently receiving Holy Communion, so much so that the nuns would often cluck their tongues at this family presumptuous enough to believe they were that worthy.*

*In a family that eventually produced two other priests and two nuns, it was not surprising that Francis wanted to study for the priesthood. For many the seminary in 1924 was considered a vehicle — to the priesthood, and to social status for those who came out of huge working-class families. As Francis studied to be a priest, the talk around the seminary was divided between God and mammon, the latter getting more interest as men approached ordination. Who would get the wealthy parishes with the generous Mass stipends that would provide a monthly bonus exceeding monthly pay? Who would go to the influential monsignor's parish and begin the climb into church hierarchy and administration?*

Francis sounded a sour note in the choir of voices raised up to status, money, power. He wasn't a model seminarian, often late for Rosary or Mass. His grades were among the best, but his awareness of the world outside was off key. Francis could not forget the working-class people. Yet his classmates clamored to serve the men in starched white collars and the women whose hands were not red and roughened like those of his mother and her friends in his old neighborhood.

Avoiding the cultic high-priest role from the start, Father Francis Eschweiler began to form small discussion groups in his first parish, trying to translate to the common man the church's little-used but strong historical background of a social action philosophy. As he was moved from parish to parish — often at the request of fellow priests — he grew stronger in his belief that the Catholic lay person had to be helped not only in spiritual but in temporal matters. He worked with labor organizers and leaders and was branded a socialist for advocating such outlandish acts as a minimum wage law. When his affiliation with union men became too much for the church to bear he was banished to a rural parish where he reached the bleakest moments of his priestly life.

In 1957, at the age of forty-eight, when he was allowed to start a church in a developing suburban area, he sensed that even more drastic changes were coming to Catholicism and that new kinds of structures were going to be required. He had no bylaws to conform to, so he and the people of the Good Shepherd Congregation created their own traditions. The old stipend system was thrown out and creative liturgy introduced. Small groups proliferated. A simple but utilitarian building was constructed that foreshadowed the changes in worship that Vatican II would foster.

Today Fran, or Frannie as everybody calls him, is sixty-four years old. He wears plaid sports jackets and deep-colored shirts and resembles a science teacher more than a priest. When in his car, the cassette player is plugged in and the words of a theologian or philosopher fill the air. He jogs a nine-minute mile five times a week; he swims in cold Wisconsin lakes; he dreads the thought of retirement. Thirty-eight years a priest, and his message has essentially not changed.

A parish of Europeans — Hungarians, Austrians, Slavs — at the height of the Depression. Yes, Milwaukee's St. Michael's was a parish of very poor people. Men were out of work, families hungry; it was a time of discontent in America. People were wondering how everything could have gone so wrong. And so was I. And where was the church while all this went on? In the seminary, when I heard about social action from men like Monsignors Francis Haas and John Ryan, it always appeared to me that that was what priests ought to be doing. All this business of just putting oil and water over people and saying certain words, of limiting ministry exclusively to ritual never had much meaning for me.

As the new priest at St. Michael's I was given church groups like sodalities and the Holy Name Society, and from the beginning I was inclined to put little emphasis on social events and more on social action. In those days social action was outlined pretty nicely in the encyclicals *Rerum Novarum* and *Quadragesimo Anno,* and I'd try to explain these to the men. The radicals and Communists were going at them pretty heavy and these men were ready to listen. Many lived in shacks and they were ready to jump onto anything that promised a better way of life.

I talked about the dignity of man and how his personhood was being violated, that he had no voice in the government of his life, no voice in industry. We had political democracy and freedom, but the workingman had not established his economic democracy. I told the men they would never get their dignity unless they were organized, because the other side was organized against them and if they had to slug it out in the competitive jungle they had better be at least at equal strength.

Although those two social action encyclicals were the pride of the church, too few people talked about them and too few of the church members knew about them. I think a lot of people were surprised that a priest could have any sensitivity toward the day-to-day plight of the workingman. We were supposed to be involved with higher things, things of the spirit.

My pastor at St. Michael's saw enough poverty around, so while he wasn't really enthusiastic about what I was doing he didn't try to stop me. But there were rumors that I was a Commie or a socialist, a rabble rouser. The men I lived with in the rectory felt that the priority in the priest's job was to expand the church sodalities, get the numbers. I believed in small groups, study clubs or discussion groups and that type of thing. I was eased out of St. Michael's because of those differences in philosophy. Plurality wasn't a word we had even heard about in those days.

By today's standards my views are common, accepted. Back in 1937, when I said that the Mass is not a prayer, it is an action, they thought I was a heretic. I always said it was a proclamation of what we believed in and tried to live out, not some isolated rite. Hell, they thought this Fran guy was really off his rocker.

I was an assistant in three places, but I can't say my ministry changed that much during those moves. I learned a lot, but my view was pretty clear-cut: the workingman needed help and I could give it, I felt. I conducted what was known in those days as "labor schools." I went to the blue-collar workers and taught them what to expect when they were part of a bargaining committee and how to handle themselves. I'd work with guys who were organizing and developing unions and just try to give them the Christian ammunition, the basis of good Catholic action as enunciated by the two encyclicals. It was all there: when private initiative fails to meet the needs of people for the common good, it is the right and even the duty of the government to intervene. That would justify minimum wage laws and the Wagner Act, which the big companies hooted were vestiges of socialism. Too often the church was just as vested an interest, and they weren't at the forefront of workers' rights. Somehow the church didn't trust the little man to do or set anything right; somehow he needed some greater authority to dictate to him.

I'm a fighter by nature, but I wear big padded gloves. I never really felt enraged by the priests who stayed in their rectories answering the door and telephone in a kind of "fire station" operation. They didn't want to get their fingernails dirty, but I didn't mind. I just thought that I, this priest, had to do what I could do to get people where they were and relate to them where their greatest needs and problems were. Right then they needed jobs and a decent standard of living. I thought that Christ would never be visible to them unless a priest would really be the kind of man who would show compassion and understanding for their problems and not just gloss everything over with a plenary indulgence.

The workers liked me, I liked them. Down at the chancery they weren't that impressed. From the 1930s and through the big strike of Allis-Chalmers in 1947 there was a string of notes. "Frank, you were quoted as saying thus and so. Lay off." The Allis-Chalmers strike really got me in hot water because so many of the guys who were on the bargaining committee came to me for advice and the people downtown knew about it.

Joe Dombeck was in charge of the picket line and late one night he came to my room, and he was worried. "Going to have violence, Father," he said. "The guys are pretty itchy. They want to go into the plant and take over the machines. They are pressuring me to be violent and if I don't yield they're going someplace else for a leader."

I kept talking to Joe, trying to show him that nonviolence was the right way, and the best way in the long run. I ate beans with the men on the picket line, and I got a chance to reason with them. There was some violence, but we averted a break-in which could have really been a bloodbath.

Then it got back to the chancery that I had attended a UAW meeting and was talking to the stewards. They hit me with the fact that I hadn't gotten permission. Permission to attend a union meeting? At that time I was in the middle of a teaching year at St. Francis Seminary and suddenly I was yanked out. There was an opening and I guess I was positively the only man for the job. What it boiled down to was exile; they exiled me to a little country parish in Kewaskum, forty miles from Milwaukee. It could have been four hundred.

What sunk in and really hurt was that the church obviously was standing on the side of management and didn't want one of their boys mingling with labor types. The big money came from industry; it didn't come from the workingman. The bishop never openly confronted me about my union activities; it all came to me secondhand. But really, I was a marked man and the bigwigs wanted me out of town.

I certainly was somewhat bitter about it, but not that bitter. The bitterness was more of a surface thing. It wasn't a deep-down bitterness that made me want to hate the whole church. I said, Well, that's one dupe who doesn't know. That's not the church. But I was crushed. Plurality wasn't really a word then; neither was relevance. But that's what I was after. For me, as a minister of God, my teaching and living had to make sense to the society around me. This wasn't the Middle Ages; we couldn't just pray and think everything was going to be all right.

And they really knew how to make a guy hurt. Kewaskum wasn't just geographically removed, it was intellectually removed and culturally barren. Good honest farmers who toiled from sunup and then understandably fell asleep at meetings. Good people, but inbred and gossipy as hell. They were quite interrelated. If you stepped on one toe you hit the whole parish.

This was in the early 1950s and I tried to make the best of it. I started a dialogue Mass, but the people had a lot of trouble going with anything different from what they'd done for the past thirty years. Just simple responses in Latin and English and it made them very uncomfortable, but I wanted them to be part of the Mass. I went out on the hay wagons and threshing crews; I ate out in the fields with them. I had a few who were very loyal and whom I could work with and who were willing to be led and to develop during those years.

But those years were full of darkness and frustration. I felt like "God, my God, why have You forsaken me?" I don't want to be dramatic about it, but I had read St. John of the Cross and I felt maybe this was my "dark night." Who knows what I would have done if that had been fifteen years later when leaving the priesthood got to be an accepted thing. Many times I said the hell with this whole thing, with this wall of oppression. But I just couldn't leave the priesthood even though I felt so stymied right then. I was either stubborn, or a hardy believer!

In the years before, I was called a Commie and a socialist. In the years to follow I'd be hated for stands on open housing, I'd be condemned by the church for opposing an encyclical, but when a person feels boxed in, useless, that's the worst hurt of all. There's no way to fight back. And church officials know that, know how to take the fuse out. I can't underestimate the intellectual dryness.

Being pulled out of social activism and the excitement of the kids in the seminary and thrown out into the country where nobody read, where current events were grain prices and inches of rainfall.

Cardinal Meyer came into office and he was a more discerning man. When a couple of people in Kewaskum wrote to say this guy Eschweiler was trying to start all that new stuff out there, Meyer took that to be a good sign. He knew me from the seminary and knew I had some abilities, so he transferred me to a little better rural parish for three years. Then he called me in to ask if I'd like to be pastor of a church that didn't yet exist.

Menomonee Falls was really starting to build in 1957, and there was an obvious need for a church. I had always been damned for not keeping traditions; I figured here was the ideal opportunity to start some new traditions. Right from the start I wanted an involved kind of laity. From work in the labor movement, work in the Christian Family Movement since its inception, I saw what the so-called common man could do and how the church often passed him by as incompetent. The layman was the church and he ought to be its voice, be helped to articulate what it stood for. No priest can do that as effectively as a truly motivated layman.

We had an alfalfa field, a couple of sheds and shacks, and an old farmhouse when the diocese turned my parish over to me. The farmhouse was a stinking mess — they had had animals living in there — but we got it cleaned up and that was my home for a while. The public school wouldn't let us use their gym or facilities for services, but the theater owner said we could use the movie house on Sunday mornings. I remember one Sunday morning as I drove in for Mass, the marquee said *The Dangerous Hour.* It was good in there because it was looser, friendly, not so churchy. We had to set up the portable altar and things on the stage every week, and the guys helped out and it created the right atmosphere for the kind of church I wanted.

From the start I had an idea that Good Shepherd should not be the typical church-school combination; there were sure signs that those days were going to be over soon. I wanted more of a community, a center, a "congregation." We had lower-middle-class people who were just hanging on financially, but when the vote came up they were almost unanimous for having a school. There was time before we started building and moved in, so I took time to visit every family. It was a sort of consciousness-raising effort, to free them of the old religious views so that they could grow in a church that was going to have its own style, a relevant kind of celebration — not just hocus-pocus things in liturgy — and ministry.

As with anything new, there were moments of great doubt. The people didn't know where I was trying to lead them. Half the time I wasn't sure either. But I've never had any difficulty talking to God, and I got a lot of reinforcement from the Scripture — seeing Jesus constantly reflecting, going to the desert, bubbling up to the Father. I'd just try to share with God the experience, whether it was joyful, one of great doubt or hesitance, or one that demanded new courage. I prayed for revelation, guidance, things God concealed from the wise and revealed to the little ones. Sometimes I'd just sit in church or in my room and say, "God, what should I do?" And I could come away refreshed . . . and sometimes with an insight into what I should do.

I was a little old (forty-eight) to be starting a parish, but I had seen what worked and what didn't and I was ready for the challenge. On the organization side I forged ahead, starting two Christian Family Movement groups, leadership training for laymen, and working with lay people who helped in the services. But I cooled it at the beginning with my sermons. I had my fingers burned before for saying too much, and perhaps too soon, from the pulpit. I knew my audience was not inclined my way; they were primarily Republican and on the conservative side, but it's hard to keep your ideals hidden long. I remember one Sunday I let out the stops and said something about the public ownership of certain utilities and why should we have all kinds of milk wagons and trucks running down the same street, competing and wasting. Everybody's got to drink milk or use the telephone or have electricity. They started wondering if they didn't have a socialist in their midst.

So many people have said the real place for the church is in the slums. There's no doubt that's more dramatic, that the need there is more pressing, but the new wave of suburbanites had to have the Gospel too. I don't mean pabulum. I mean the fullness of the Gospel. So when open housing became an issue I really pushed our people to come out for it. To say our doors were open to anyone. The resistance was strong, but there were a lot of people who had seen the light and they helped balance those who kept saying, He's bringing them in, he's bringing them in.

One CFM group took up open housing and using the CFM technique — which is actually St. Thomas' prudence bit — they did the three things: observe, judge, and act. They looked over the situation, got the facts, talked to people, then faced themselves with: Is this human or right or good or bad, and then what do we do about it? They found that attitudes were so hardened that the best action they could come up with was to bring in a panel of blacks from an inner city parish who were going around and presenting the housing problems from the black man's point of view.

That meeting was considered by all of us to be a pretty moderate action, but it was a turning point for me in Menomonee Falls. The panel barely got started when a group of John Birchers got up and started screaming. They wanted to confront these people right then. The chairman told them the panel would have their dialogue first and then we'd break into smaller groups for questions. Hell, some of these people hadn't ever talked to a black person. The CFM group had found hardened racism and prejudice and a lot of stupidity. White people didn't think blacks ate like them. It was weird the ideas they had.

The meeting went to the verge of being a violent thing. There was shouting and pushing and shoving, and that all got to the chancery. Then the rumors began to fly. I was trying to bring black people out there to live, and that would reduce property values. I had taken parish money and bought property across the street for low-cost apartments to bring in the blacks. A number of families left to join other parishes. Some thought I was imprudent and tactless. Good pastors are real diplomats and don't lose parishioners. Why did I always have to stir the waters? And be a trouble-maker? The chancery reminded me of the departing parishioners, of the "trouble" I was causing in "River City." But through all that I felt tranquil. If I was in trouble for this, I thought, so be it!

There were enough people on my side who saw what I was trying to do, and the numbers of people who came to us kept growing. Parish boundaries didn't mean anything any more and the people who came came because our church offered something different. In fact we have more than two hundred families from the metropolitan Milwaukee area who are now members. There's a joke around that there's a Roman Catholic church, a Catholic church, and a Christian church, and people can take their choice. We're the Christian church.

Vatican II put an emphasis on collegiality, the principle of the layman and the clergy working together, sharing authority, each having a voice and neither controlling the other. There was collegiality in our church from the start. Lay people were given responsibility, they were readers in the liturgy, we had singing at Mass and dialogue Mass. And a really important point: Our laymen began to see their religious belief not just as something they expressed in church but which had to be taken into the community, into their daily lives.

I wouldn't say I flaunted doing things in those days that were not approved. Let's put it this way: I went as far as I possibly could under the restrictions and perhaps once in a while I leaned on the restrictions too hard for what I believed was the good of the church. So when Vatican II came along, it wasn't like a floodgate of new things being opened to us. Vatican II just validated a lot of things we were doing all along.

I was in my fifties when Vatican II occurred, and most priests my age were threatened by it, fought it. Our training had never demanded that we update, never really demanded we re-evaluate things and chart new courses. Then Vatican II required new and developing theology, new thinking, and many of the men my age weren't capable of coping with the challenge to change. They were threatened by the thought of laymen taking over positions of power and even handling the money, which, next to the host, was to them the most sacred thing. I felt that my role was secure, because while the power of the priest was now a thing to be shared — the exercise of power was never "my thing" anyway — nevertheless people still needed the "Word" and we didn't have too many people around trained to give the Word.

Vatican II just seemed to make life a lot easier for me. Looking back, I can call the last ten years of my ministry the most exhilarating. About five years ago I dropped Confession before First Communion and was very careful to validate my position from the pulpit. That's common practice now, but then it was something. Psychologically it didn't make sense to pretend to have a child seven years old relating to God on that kind of a profound level. Sin involves a relationship with God and neighbor, either cooling it or breaking it, and I just didn't feel children of that age were mature enough to enter that kind of relationship with anybody; and they certainly weren't capable of walking out on God or even consciously offending Him.

There were some calls to the chancery and the chancery told me I had to take back what I said. I asked why, and I was told there was some directive on it. I said I knew of no law about compulsory Confession for children and I'd done some reading on the history of Confession and I didn't see the need for it at that age. I told them the official church could always find a directive someplace to cover any instance of anything and that I wasn't going to change. They never pushed me on the point again. I think priests quit too easily sometimes. All you have to do is lean on the door and it opens.

I really tried not to duck issues as they came up in my ministry — from open housing to Confession. I didn't always do right, but I did something. And for an old clerical codger, I was questioned now and then by the media about the church's stance on this or that. When *Humanae Vitae* came out and I opposed it in favor of personal conscience in reference to a responsible use of contraception in marriage, a television reporter did an interview in my living room and really gave me a loaded question. It went something like "Father Eschweiler, it's known that you've taken a position that people have the freedom to form their own conscience regarding birth control. How is it that other priests haven't taken that stand?"

The camera was running; I didn't have time to think. So I did say, "I can't speak for other priests, but maybe they haven't done the necessary reading that a priest ought to be doing to keep current on a subject like this. And some of the best theologians —

with all due respect to the Pope — have said that we need to respect the consciences of responsible people in this matter, that it is our pastoral duty to provide them with moral guidelines that will help them to a right conscience in this matter of family limitation." I said, "Vatican II clearly equated the importance of conjugal love along with the procreative purpose of marriage, and how are you able to sustain that if you have no option except the precarious practice of rhythm or simply total abstinence if you concluded that having more children would be irresponsible in your case?"

Personal conscience wasn't a new issue, I maintained. Vatican II had clearly stated that parents alone had to make the decision about how many children they should have in view of their economic situation, the physical and mental health of the mother, even the total good of the community. As I became more aware of what was really involved in bearing and raising children, as I listened to parents grappling with this problem, my views changed through the years until I got to the point where I made no yes or no judgment on contraceptives. I gave couples the guidelines and asked them to make up their minds. I told them that I felt there were people who in given instances certainly were morally permitted to prevent conception unnaturally, but that each couple had to come to grips with their own conscience in this matter and come to a personal Christian decision about what would constitute responsible parenthood in their situation.

I knew it would be only a matter of time for some kind of reaction from the chancery after the interview. "Dear Frank: Don't put us priests all in the same category. We're not all that stupid and it's imprudent of you to try and speak for the church and diocese. This is the official position of the church and how can you differ with that?" So the chancery says all priests aren't stupid — and I know that — but then they fall back on doctrine for a rebuttal.

So I wrote back. The fellow who had to write on behalf of the chancery is really a good boy; I had him in seminary. I said that I didn't mean to impugn all the clergy or their intelligence but I felt many hadn't done their homework, so they didn't know there were any options other than the old hard line. And I said Pope

Paul had kind of retracted what Vatican II had gone forward with in the vision of what marriage ought to be.

There were the usual hate letters too, most of them unsigned and irrational. But the letter that hurt the most was from the pastor of my parish where I went to school and celebrated my first Mass. *"Sentire cum Ecclesia,"* he said, "think and feel with the church, Frank." It's an old expression we used in the seminary. If you thought and felt with the church and were an obedient son, that was the ultimate. And then he resorted to a familiar, sentimental, and hackneyed cliché: "Your dear mother would be upset in her grave if she knew."

When you're younger you wonder if you aren't crazy sometimes because you're out there alone. And when you're older you still question your sanity. Maybe I'm tactless, because I am always getting in trouble. I had my faculties taken away once when I was confessor to sisters in a convent. I was doing some counseling and the mother superior wrote the bishop that this man was unsettling the community with his conferences. And the nuns were running over to his room for "counseling." If I was to do it over again I wouldn't have spent so much time with some of those nuns. What I mean is, many of them were more sick than sinning. Maybe I was imprudent, but at any rate my intentions were honest. What they wanted was a friend mostly. That was a bad word too — "friend" — because PF's, i.e., "particular friendships," in those days were taboo. Even worse, they told the superior I helped them. But again, how to come to grips with a woman who is frustrated, unhappy about her life? Turn her out with two Hail Marys, or try to make some sense out of her life, tie it in to what the Gospel is telling each of us. The prevailing and accepted practice at that time would turn her out with two Hail Marys and not get "involved." The curt letter followed from the chancery: "Your faculties for hearing Sisters' Confessions are hereby suspended." No explanation. That's oppressive, that's stifling, and it hurts. And you say to yourself many times that you've had it. But for me it always seemed like things opened up. That new opportunities presented themselves if I had the patience to stick around. I think many of the men who have left gave up too quickly. They weren't willing to wait and lean on the door, wait some more and lean some more. I found it works. The door keeps opening further and further.

When I look back to see what really kept me in and functioning I always end up saying "people." Lay groups like the Christian Family Movement — and I've been in that for twenty-seven years — gave me the feeling that I was getting through. Given the opportunity, the Spirit could really work in these groups, transform these people. Five or six couples and I sitting around in a CFM group, in a home, exploring our faith, trying to find out what God is summoning us to do in one facet of our lives. Maybe we'd take a problem like race relations and after carefully observing and judging on the matter the people would realize they really couldn't go on calling themselves Christians and still harbor these hatreds, and they had to do something positive about it. Or in their marriages, they had to start really loving or caring for that person right next to them. CFM helped me to save my own soul and my priesthood, really. Without some tangible evidence that what I stood for and talked about was being understood and incorporated in a few lives I never could have gone on. While I was nourishing them with the Word which gives life, they were giving me hope.

This is the church, these people, and this is worth working for, and struggling for as a priest, not PRIEST. I feel that this is the people business at the highest, deepest, most profound level. Where men and God meet, and I'm the coordinator of that. I help create a condition whereby the two can come together, where people can experience the "Good News" and realize the fullness of God, where they can come to the Father by coming into contact with the humanity of Jesus.

I can't think of any other place where I could be as effective in reaching these people at such a level. I don't regard my commitment to the formal church as something mandatory simply because of my vows. Vows after all will never hold a man together when the ground from under gives way. It's something else that is instinctive, something so deeply embedded in my faith, so firmly rooted in the core of my person, that somehow the Spirit calls me to work this way, even with a structure that too often is immobile, intransigent, and impervious to any kind of change. I'd like to think with St. Paul that it is the "love of Christ" that "drives me on."

A word about institutions. I feel with Gregory Baum that all institutions — whether it's the Catholic Church, General Motors, the National Association of Manufacturers, or the government with its bureaucracies — have built-in "Pathologies" which make them turn in on themselves and by gradual erosion turn away from the purposes for which they were originally established. Once "established," they become blind to the needs and demands of the people they were intended to serve. They become hidebound and insensitive to persons. They become impersonal and defensive as they become big. The "bigger" and more powerful they get, the more they turn their energies to self-preservation of the institution rather than to the service of persons. It is a kind of institutional sickness which plagues them and makes them paralytic, unable to "move." Any suggestions for change are put down as dangerous, subversive, and destructive of that sacred cow which we call "law and order."

But for all their flaws and weaknesses, institutions are not only here to stay, they are necessary and viable structures within which men are called to grow and work. We cannot live without them. Since they are always in need of reform it is imperative that people with charisma or leadership dynamics stay in to bring about the necessary evolution of change and reform from within — to keep the institution honest and human and sensitive to its true purposes. And in this way ultimately create a new institution.

The only alternative I see to this is to jump over the wall — to drop out. Maybe we need a few people to do this — to witness to the corruption of the existing establishment, to point up the need for radical change. But to cop out is generally to be alone, alienated, on one's own. I for one can't work out there alone, by myself. To me the church, the priesthood, is still the frame of reference I need to work from. I'll bypass the rigamarole, the excess baggage, the needless paraphernalia which the simple structure that Jesus instituted did not include. Frankly, I have a quarrel with some of the priests who have decided to drop out and, I believe, who have quit too soon. Many of them were precisely the kind of charismatic men who abandoned the "sinking ship" when they were most needed. And some of them, it seems to me, have been less than honest in stating upon their leaving that they were embarking upon some new and more productive "ministry out there" — free from the inhibiting and stifling roadblocks that the institutional church put in their way. I just haven't seen any significant, exciting new ministries that have emerged in the promised land out there. Mostly they are married, and I have no quarrel with that call if that's what it is, and maybe that's "ministry" enough for them. But let's not call it by another name.

I feel bad about the many good young men who have left, and I wish them the best. Some of them who have worked with me have helped to free me. I wish they had seen fit to bypass the peripheral elements within the structure while remaining faithful to the substance of the church.

I still think the priest has great power. I think he can have a persuasive influence — in the right sense, not manipulating people, not swarming all over them — and lead them to freedom. There are such great opportunities to completely free people from their inadequacies, fears, hangups, and bring out the best potential. Like Jesus did, a priest can draw people out.

And I'm not trying to make a case for those priests who just stay in, many of whom are already dead but just not yet buried. I make a plea for men to stay in creatively, who will be true to themselves, moving as their conscience tells them to move, and being responsive to the Spirit. We stifle the Spirit every day, all of us do, because we get our knuckles rapped. If enough people believe in change and improving the quality of life in the Church, the structure will change in due time. We found that out here at Good Shepherd.

I try to keep my eyes on Jesus. He was so strong, and yet so human. He always kept on coming, and yet he needed help, and asked for it. Not only from his Father, but from his friends. "Sit down here and watch with me," he pleaded. "My soul is sad unto death." I would hope that priests generally, and young priests in particular, would ponder deeply these words in the Transfiguration account in Mark's gospel: ". . . looking around they no longer saw anyone with them — only Jesus." A priest will keep a right perspective by fixing his eyes on Jesus. He is our "Way." Also our "Way out" of frustration and despair. No doubt optional celibacy is important and will open new doors for many to find fulfillment in their ministry. But I have a nagging feeling that the "marriage thing," which is quite a demanding ministry by itself, will not free the priest for all the kinds of fulfillment that he is really looking for — nor from the impediments, hangups, and frustrations that establishments impose. Like all people, the priest needs to be loved and he wants to succeed. And all of us, priests and lay people, must find all kinds of ways to give him the love that humanly he needs and help him to reach that measure of success in his ministry that he must have if he is to experience a sense of fulfillment and well-being as a person and a priest. Let's face it, lack of success can be a priest's problem, unless his faith is deep and he doesn't expect too much tangible evidence of success. The parable of the seed says a lot to me. Most of it fell on ground that wouldn't receive it. What the hell success did Jesus have? Twelve guys he spent three years on, and they weren't that solidly faithful. We priests are human and we have to see some signs that some seeds are taking root. I admit to my own lack of faith in this regard, always wanting things to germinate overnight. I think we should wait a "week"! But if you are true to yourself you really can't lose. You may look like a loser for ten or more years, but ultimately the day of vindication comes.

I am staying around — and have stayed around — because I'm tenacious, but also I'm a hopeful man. If I abandon the ship, then a lot of others will take over the wheel, and places like Good Shepherd might not be. We are an island here, an option, a center. We are not a geographical parish. We serve hundreds of people from all over the area who are drawn here because they find something that is credible, that makes sense. We need a multiplication of different kinds of islands today to meet the varied needs of people, not just mimeographed parishes all doing the same thing. While we hang in here and stay on deck — where "the Spirit breathes where He will" and manifests Himself in a variety of styles of ministry and worship — we at Good Shepherd are proud to be, to quote a few phrases from our "Parish Philosophy,"

*A happening that is*
*always happening,*
*where the Word goes out*
*that God is Love*
*and all is well . . .*
*A* CONGREGATION *of people*
*who gather and sing*
*because they believe the news*
*is good . . .*
*where there is always a meal*
*at which to drink "new wine"*
*. . . where reconciliation and forgiveness*
*are always a* CELEBRATION.

We are proud to serve the church at large by being responsibly different as we respond to the Spirit in being

*a fellowship of believers*
*who seek always to be open to*
*and listening to the Spirit*
*as He speaks to us*
*and summons us*
*to see new visions,*
*to chart new courses,*
*and to accept new challenges*
*which enable us to grow.*
*and develop*
*and become whole.*

At least we've done something "to make all things new," and it's been exciting, serving people who want and need more than carbon copy ministry — and it's been worth staying in for.

I'm hopeful. Last week we had a meeting of thirty interested priests who work together to create good liturgy. I helped start the group, and those men by their attendance and interest give me hope. And we give hope to one another. And they'll push out in new directions and they're not going to be stymied or hampered. And that courage reinforces an old hand like me to stay around for a while.

**FIRE**

# The Laity: More Than Functionaries and Activists

April 8, 1986

Ruminating through *CRUX OF THE NEWS,* a weekly newsletter and gold mine of information for people who work in the Church, almost always provides rich news bits about life in a Church on the move. Here's a point I can identify with, perhaps more than many a priest or lay person can. It's about lay formation, which, to those who know me, has always been a "thing" with me. It's evidence of the pastor in me that keeps bubbling up.

Vatican II emphasized the role of the laity in the Church because they have gifts to offer which, if not called forth and utilized, will be a loss to the Church. It has often occurred to me that in general we have been somewhat cavalier in engaging the people of God to minister without giving them adequate formation. At times we haven't even given them boot-camp fundamentals about the nature of the Church and her mission, about collegiality, the centrality of Liturgy in the life of the Church, the power of the Word, the urgency of an ecumenical approach in all of our ministry, and the need for a profound prayer life.

Here are some observations from a plenary meeting of the Pontifical Council for Laity held in Rome in 1985: "Lay formation," they find, "is virtually nonexistent at parish and diocesan levels." There is a "pressing need," they say, to teach various groups at all levels of the Church (clergy, laity, religious, and movements) to collaborate with each other. Then they add that similar formation programs are needed for the clergy. To which I add, AMEN!

There's no substitute for competence, technical and spiritual, in the Church.

As the priest shortage increases, the priest needs to give top priority to **formation** of lay people. There's no cheap alternative. Simply appointing individuals and committees to perform tasks and then turning them loose will not do. In the reign of God we need more than functionaries and activists. We need people who first "hear the Word," that is, assimilate the mind and spirit of Christ, and then become "doers of the Word."

Based on my personal experience, the priest of today will need more than ever to be first of all a **minister of the Word** and then a **prophetic leader** who builds up the community, not by dominating, but by serving; not by barking out orders or simply doling out assignments, but by working collegially — which is to say, by listening (because the Spirit speaks in all!), by engaging in prayerful discussion, and by coming to decisions through discernment and consensus. The priest must ever be the catalyst, the enabler who calls forth the people's gifts and then provides ongoing support and nurturing by encouraging, stimulating, and supplying instructive insights to groups and individuals. He is to be the "minister of ministers." His must always be a **ministry of presence.** Like Yahweh, he must always be the "I Am" person who is at hand, who is accessible, who is there to serve, to instruct, to lead, and to guide.

# The Liturgy:
# The Lord Present in Our Midst

June 13, 1986

Recently I ran across a letter written by the late Romano Guardini, a famous liturgist who sent this message to a liturgical congress shortly before he died. It was not long after the Vatican II *Constitution on the Sacred Liturgy* with its call to radical reform was issued. Guardini indicates in this letter that, as a consequence of this monumental *Constitution on the Sacred Liturgy,* there could be a real danger that we would busy ourselves with all kinds of necessary changes which would simply touch the surface and periphery of the kind of genuine renewal that is urgently needed. Much more will be required than becoming familiar with new texts and gestures, using the vernacular, singing together, and achieving the overall active participation of the people. He reminds us that what is most needed is a profound sense of awareness that when we gather for the Liturgy, we are engaging in what he calls a true liturgical act. The people gathered here are not just another collection or assembly of individuals. This is a unique kind of congregation.

When we gather to celebrate the Eucharist, we are Church. We are the Body of Christ — Saint Paul calls it the **Mystical**

Body of Christ. We are a gathering of people uniquely bonded together in a mysterious communion with our Lord and with one another the likes of which there is no other. There is nothing comparable to this Corpus, and, as we celebrate Eucharist, we need to have a deep awareness of this, along with a great desire to want to celebrate precisely this liturgical act. There must be a consciousness that Liturgy, in its etymological sense, is the work of the people, the work of God's people. The Liturgy is something we **do** and we **do together.** We come here with our bodies and our spirits, and this constitutes what we are: a congregation. As we come together, the Lord Jesus is present in our midst, and He calls us to open ourselves to Him and to each other.

The exclusive use of missalettes in which we bury ourselves and our hearts while we are looking into the texts — and in some measure also the use of hymnals — can become a barrier to our sense of being the Body of Christ and of doing something together. We come together as a people who have been called by God and who have responded to that call. The very act of joining with our brothers and sisters implies that we accept them, that there is no one's concern that is not ours. We accept the Lord before whom we stand, and we accept one another with whom we are now gathered.

It is quite possible to go through a Eucharistic Celebration that is hardly at all an authentic liturgical act. If the presider is perfunctory as he says all the right words, goes through the gestures and the actions, and recites (or drones!) the Eucharistic Prayer; if the people are simply kind of going along, making the responses; if their singing is listless and they come forth in a routine manner to take the Body of Christ and the Precious Blood in the cup, saying their "Amens" — all this can be pure ritualism without in any real sense constituting a liturgical act.

When the presider and the ministers make their procession through the church at the beginning of the Eucharist, there ought to be a sense that here and now the Lord Jesus is present in our midst and is calling us to make a conscious effort to be in turn present to Him and to each other. This already is prayer. There is no need to conjure up all kinds of inward inspirations or meanings at this point. We should simply allow ourselves to be caught up into this liturgical act. An illustration of this might make it more clear: if we were asked, for example, to come forth at the Offertory and to bring our gifts to the House of Peace — to leave the pew and make that walk to the front of the altar and to place our gift in the basket — that action, that use of our bodies, that movement, that procession, is prayer.

Again, when at the Consecration the priest holds up the bread and the cup in his hands, he need not say any words to

---

*The very act of joining with our brothers and sisters implies that we accept them.*

---

clarify the meaning of this action. This external act is already a prayer without any accompaniment of song or words. The ritual itself should provide a clear invitation to each person present to look up with a sense of wonder, a contemplative wonder which has its roots in a deep faith, as if to say, "Here I am" before the Lord who is somehow present to me in the bread and the cup. My whole person, my entire self, is being given, is being offered.

Another example. When the presider extends his hands over the chalice and calls down the Holy Spirit in the Eucharistic Prayer, that gesture is a powerful symbol. It should be allowed to speak for itself and the people should read it as such. I remember a time at Good Shepherd when the liturgy team was planning the Palm Sunday processions. It was felt that the processions should be organized in a way that would generate better praying and singing. This was a valid concern, but the real question that should have been asked was this: How can the act of walking by the people in the procession become a true liturgical act? How can we make this a moment to experience the Lord's appearance in our midst — our Lord progressing here and now in this land of ours? We have a long way to go to infuse this kind of new life into our Liturgy. We still haven't addressed the question of the nature of genuine liturgical actions as opposed to other ordinary religious actions of personal piety and individual devotion.

There are some promising related developments in our contemporary theology that could be helpful in coming to such an understanding. Today we are much more interested in what it means to be Church. Today, too, we have a more precise understanding of our being a people whose bodies and spirits, whose outward and inward personas, form one integrated whole.

In our liturgical renewal we have much to learn from these developments. But we will need much more than intellectual head-trip explanations. More rationalizing will not serve our purpose. The faculties of looking and of doing and of shaping will have to be sharpened. Liturgical music must be more than merely decorative and peripheral. Its sounds and words must be integral to the liturgical action. Carefully selected renditions with good biblical words and spirited singing are indispensable to prayerful worship. The gathered people are more than a collection of persons who are sitting together. Their presence is not simply spatial. They are a solidarity of people. They are the people of God, the Body of Christ. We pray for the day when this profound understanding of who we are and what we are really doing in our Sunday Eucharist — of what constitutes the liturgical act — will be understood.

# Graced Moments:
# God Present in Daily Living

June 22, 1986

Some reflections on my annual priests' retreat. The retreat master talked last night about what he called "graced moments" in our lives — moments when God is revealed to us in significant ways.

In Vatican II's *Dogmatic Constitution on Divine Revelation* we are told that God is revealed in two ways: in Jesus and in created reality. In the famous novel *The Color Purple,* Celie and Shug talk about how they do not find God in church when they go there, but experience God in themselves before they go to church and then take God to church and share the God they already possess. They call to mind the profound truth that religious experience is not limited exclusively to sacred settings. Indeed, it might be said that unless we have allowed God to possess us in ordinary day-to-day life situations, we are not likely to experience a God-revealing action in the houses of our worship.

Graced moments are seldom the burning-bush type that Moses enjoyed or the extraordinary out-of-this-world encounters such as Saint Paul had on the road to Damascus. While graced moments can and do happen in sacraments and liturgical celebrations, they will not be accompanied by thundering from the heavens and blinding conversion experiences. They will happen more often in created reality, in dialogue, in relationships, in public gatherings, in places where people play and work and sing and suffer and struggle. The death-resurrection of Jesus has unleashed a power and an energy that is everywhere operative in the universe.

The presence of God is felt by all of us in the awesomeness of a flaming sunset, the sounds of rushing water at Niagara Falls, the rhythmic patter of rain on a roof as we lie quietly in our beds at night. The anguished scream of a birthing mother followed by the initial cry of a newborn baby are like the two sides of a death-resurrection experience. These are graced moments which provide a kind of Liturgy of the Word in which God chooses to speak to us in the sacrament of the present moment.

On a personal note, there was a time in my life when I went through a period of deep anxiety. I suddenly became aware of how vulnerable and weak I was. I had thought that I knew how to pray, but only in my great need did I begin to truly turn to God. For the first time I discovered what it really meant to encounter Jesus in a personal way. Only after months of struggle and darkness did I come to this. It was a painful period in which God seemed to abandon and desert me. It was also a turning point in my life — a graced time which made me see how insufficient I was. I learned what it meant to be dependent and, with that, my trust in Jesus began to grow measurably. I conclude now that whatever gift I have as a priest to touch people is pure gift because I was first touched by Him.

Saint Paul tells us: " . . . for when I am weak, then I am strong" and "power is made perfect in weakness" (2 Corinthians 12:9-10). In an age of narcissism it is difficult to comprehend Paul's paradox that in our relationship with the transcendent, it is precisely in our weakness that we become instruments of strength. It is in our brokenness that God comes to our rescue. Saint Peter puts it well:

> "God opposes the proud
> but bestows favor on the humble."
>
> 1 Peter 5:5

This experience is shared by many, and I am grateful to be one of them.

# The Pain
# of Having No Burden

August 3, 1986

These are some reflections on Luke 12:13-21.

Someone in the crowd says to Jesus, "Teacher, tell my brother to give me my share of our inheritance." Sounds like another parable of the prodigal son, someone asking for his inheritance money so he can spend it in reckless living. Jesus doesn't answer the question directly. He says, "Friend, who has set me up as your judge or arbiter?" In other words, He is saying that it's not for Him to settle their family squabbles. Jesus senses that there is more to the man's question to which He has to respond. He gives us a marvelous little sentence in which He denounces that acquisitive spirit which places such exaggerated value on the accumulation of material things: "Avoid greed in all its forms. A [person] may be wealthy, but . . . possessions do not guarantee . . . life" (Luke 12:15). All the wealth in the world, He is suggesting, all the security that derives from gratifying our appetite for things, is not going to satisfy the deepest hunger of the human spirit.

At the core of the human psyche there is an urgent need for significance in our lives. We need to give ourselves to a cause that takes us beyond meeting our own personal needs.

An ancient Jewish tale tells of a young woman who approaches an old woman with the question, "Old woman, what is life's heaviest burden?" The old woman replies, "The heaviest burden in life is not to have any burden to carry at all."

A wise old man once said, "The purpose of life is not to be happy, but the purpose of life is to matter so that when our life has been lived, we will know that we have made a difference." To carry a burden is to matter and to make a difference.

Dr. Viktor Frankl, the famous German psychoanalyst who was imprisoned in a Nazi concentration camp for several years, tells about his experiences in that camp in a remarkable little book, *A Search for Meaning.* He and the other inmates were subjected to all sorts of dehumanizing indignities to break their spirits. Many of his peers in prison buckled under the pressure and suffered breakdowns resulting from the torture and mistreatment. They could not find sufficient meaning in their lives. For lack of purpose they despaired and died prematurely. In the midst of such torture, Dr. Frankl struggled with all his soul to sustain his spirit and to find reasons to want to continue living.

In the prison yard one day Dr. Frankl saw a beautiful bird perched on the top of a shovel standing against the wall. It was singing beautifully, as birds do in the early morning hours. He thought about the beauty of God's creation — about trees and flowers and water, animals and children, smiling faces, and voices of people who are joyful. He thought about relationships, his family, wife, friends, persons who needed him and were waiting for him to come back to them. Seeing the bird made him want to cling to life in spite of the threatening and deathly situation surrounding him. Dr. Frankl is convinced that many mentally ill people, especially the suicidal, are people living their lives without substantive meaning that will justify their wanting to live.

I sometimes wonder if the frequency of midlife crises in our society can be traced to an exaggerated concern for personal fulfillment — wanting to be Number One — or with the social climbing which often includes a lust for possessions. "There's got to be more out there," they say, "and I want to achieve it." It may just be that what they are really hungering for will be found in the Gospel value of Jesus, expressed in the words, "A [person] may be wealthy, but . . . possessions do not guarantee . . . life." That is to say, possessions do not guarantee a life that is significant — a life that allows the ego to cross over to the Other.

The old woman was right. Having nothing to carry at all is a greater burden than carrying what you presently think is too heavy for you. To be without conscience, for example, at this moment in history when nations are stockpiling weapons capable of annihilating our planet and to make no attempt to say "no" is to be weighed down and burdened in the depths of the soul. The pain of not being able to scream in the middle of a nightmare, to go through life without a sense of obligation, is a galling burden. Life becomes perfectly meaningless once we are convinced that nothing we do can make a difference. The purpose of life indeed is to matter. Possessions do not guarantee life.

**FIRE**

# Easter: Then and Now

May, 1988

Easter is always more than what we say about it. Easter defies explanation. Collect all the descriptive adjectives you will, all the well-chosen and appropriate nouns, and all the pertinent predicates you can find, throw them all together and you will not articulate the true meaning of that incomparable event which stands at the center of human history — Jesus' resurrection. And ours!

Easter is something you have to experience. You have to take hold of it and allow the transforming power of the Risen Lord to seep into the depths of your person even as the ecstatic Saint Paul did on that memorable day when he encountered the Risen Jesus on the road to Damascus. Paul had never seen the historical Jesus, but that one mystical and transfiguring experience of the Risen One had so radically changed his life that shortly before his death he was able to cry out: ". . . I live, no longer I, but Christ lives in me" (Galatians 2:20). In the full glow of that resurrected life which encompassed his whole being Paul was able to exclaim triumphantly: "For I am convinced that neither death, nor life . . . nor present things, nor future things . . . will be able to separate us from the love of God in Christ Jesus, our Lord" (Romans 8:38-39).

A long-held concept which situated the death of Jesus at the center of the salvation event has been rightly replaced with a contemporary theology of the Paschal Mystery, that is, the combined death-resurrection of Jesus as the cause of our redemption. In this view, the death of Jesus is no longer seen as the all-important climax of His life and mission, and the Easter event as merely a kind of necessary appendix establishing once and for all His divinity. The death and resurrection of Jesus are inseparable. Good Friday and Easter are one reality. The seed of Jesus' death planted on Calvary's hill is the direct cause of that rich harvest which is the Easter triumph.

The Gospels give a clear implication that in the plan of God this was the proper sequence. We have repeated reminders that somehow Jesus **had** to die precisely in order to resurrect. ". . . unless a grain of wheat falls to the ground and dies," Jesus assures us, there will be no redemptive fruit (John 12:24). In some of the Gospel passages, there is even a note of eagerness to get on with His death. "Behold, we are going up to Jerusalem," He tells His disciples, "and the Son of Man will be . . . crucified, and he will be raised on the third day" (Matthew 20:18-19). The words suggest that this death march would be a necessary precondition for coming to glory and resurrection. "Get up, let us go," He says to His disciples as the soldiers come to apprehend Him in the garden (Matthew 26:46). The words resemble a battle cry which gives the certain promise of future triumph. To the doubting disciples on the way to Emmaus He gives this sharp rebuke for their unbelief: "Oh, how foolish you are! How slow of heart to believe. . . . Was it not **necessary** that the Messiah should suffer these things and enter into his glory?" (Luke 24:25-26, emphasis added).

Cross and crown are seen as one piece — two sides of a

single coin. The resurrection of Jesus is not simply an event which comes after the death of Jesus, but precisely **from** and **out of** His death. The death of Jesus is the very stuff of resurrection. Because Jesus was "obedient to death," Paul concluded that God "greatly exalted him," that is, raised Him up (Philippians 2:8-9). Interestingly, in John's theology being "lifted up" implies a dual raising — on the cross and from the tomb (see John 3:14). In Paul's cryptic language, in Jesus "Death is swallowed up in victory" (1 Corinthians 15:54).

Scripture scholars warn that it is idle to speculate about what exactly happened at the tomb on that memorable Sunday morning because there were no witnesses to the actual event. All we have is after-the-fact accounts of the resurrection from

---

*Unlike Lazarus . . . Jesus does not return to more of the same kind of life.*

---

believers whose testimony could hardly be regarded as objective. There were no on-camera reporters from the Jerusalem Journal at the grave site asking us to stand by for the complete report. Nor were the early Christians as preoccupied as we are with the need for on-site empirical evidence of what happened to the corpse. What is abundantly clear from the New Testament accounts is that in the resurrection something indescribably significant happened to the person of Jesus.

The post-resurrection accounts are many and conflicting, but there is total agreement that "He is risen" and that whatever happened was much more than mere resuscitation of a human corpse. The risen Jesus whom the disciples try to describe when they excitedly exclaim "We have seen the Lord" is radically changed in the core of His person. He is totally a new creation. Unlike Lazarus, who died and was then restored to the life he had previously experienced, Jesus does not return to more of the same kind of life He previously enjoyed. He is raised to a new life, fully glorified and transcended, which He describes as a life of "being with the Father." The heavenly messenger at the tomb asks the women why they are seeking Jesus here in the cemetery. "He has been raised; he is not here ... He is going before you to Galilee," they are told (Mark 16:6-7).

The Jesus who is announced as risen does indeed go before His disciples, and they seem to be variously frightened or overcome with joy as they experience Him now in a way that leaves them both confused and completely transformed. He needs some getting used to as He makes those sudden appearances which are quickly followed by equally sudden disappearances. He eats and drinks with them as He did before, but things are clearly not the same. Jesus is raised, as Paul puts it, in a way that defies description. It would seem that the creative and loving power of God, which brought all things into being in the beginning, is now doing a repeat performance in a mysterious new creation.

We are talking here of new dimensions of existence which transcend space and time. God is not held to such limits. We need new words here to describe a new life that is beyond space and time and history. Perhaps we could call it *metahistory*. We know of this profound reality only because its effects make themselves felt in our history — in our space and time, in our own lives. The Gospel puts it simply: "Jesus came and stood in their [the disciples'] midst" (John 20:19).

Something obviously happened also to the disciples. How else explain the newfound energy that enabled them to go forth even into hostile territory, fearlessly proclaiming the Good News? How else account for the rapid spread of the

Gospel and the early establishment of the structure of the Church? Skeptics who suggest that the disciples fabricated the resurrection story in order to win converts to their religious cult will have to explain the wide diversity of accounts in the four Gospels. There is clearly no collusion. Their stories simply don't jibe. This makes them all the more believable.

What is critical is that the disciples were changed. The new life that possessed them allowed them to accept untold suffering, persecution, and even martyrdom. People do not perform such heroics on the basis of wishful thinking and flimsy evidence. The resurrection was obviously an extraordinary event which profoundly shaped their lives — and ours, too.

Yes, we say the words easily enough. Resurrection shapes our lives. But when and how do we experience resurrection now? We seem quite comfortable with keeping resurrection at more than arm's length — as something that happened exclusively to Jesus in the environs of Jerusalem and Galilee some twenty centuries ago. We see it as a past event buried in history — an event which also had a profound effect on those believing disciples who in some mysterious way encountered Him, ate with Him, spoke to and listened to Him after He was raised up. But for us, the event is limited to the realm of thought. Of course, it is our firm belief that one day we, too, will be raised up in the resurrection of the body, "on the last day," we hasten to add.

For our purposes, then, resurrection is a reality that is remotely relegated to the past and the future which, at best, are areas of speculation. But what about resurrection in the present, in the here and now, in the grit and grime that marks so much of our daily living? When Jesus reminds Martha that her dead brother Lazarus will rise again, He hastens to assure her that He is talking about resurrection now. "I **am** the resurrection and the life," He tells her (John 11:25, emphasis added).

If resurrection is something that happens to us now, how are we to identify it? How will we know that it has happened, or is happening? What are the signs of its coming?

The enfleshment of Jesus in human history, identifying Himself as He did with the ordinariness of our common humanity, should be a clear sign of how God will choose to raise us up. We will not be suddenly lifted out of the tears and dirt and sweat of ordinary life into some extraterrestrial heaven where all is calm and serene. The miracles of resurrection will generally occur to us just as we are, quietly and unobtrusively, in the routine of everyday life. When it happens, we may be quite unaware of its creative power. We will not be conscious of having listened to the voice of the Eternal Word. Only later will come the discovery that we have been raised to newness of life. Only then will we recognize that a whole new vitality, a new power and energy has taken hold of us, and we have been lifted up from a situation that can only be described as death. Here are some concrete examples:

After being married for more than twenty years, Jim and Sue find that something is happening to their union. In their earlier years there was excitement in their marriage as they strove diligently to make attentive responses to each other's needs. They recognized the importance of "paying attention" and of avoiding the danger of taking each other for granted. But as Jim got more heavily involved in his work and sought fulfillment there, and as Sue focused her interests more and more on her children and a few friends, their marriage reached a dangerous plateau, and the generous love that first gave life to their union, and the surprises that are needed to keep love alive and thriving, were no longer there. Then it happened. A serious illness struck one of the children and the crisis served as a beginning to pull them together again. They sought the help of a support group in which couples experiencing a comparable situation gathered to share their burdens. Jim and Sue are presently on the road to recovering their marriage and things are on the upturn. Their relationship is not as superficially high-powered and exciting as it was in the beginning, but it is more solid, more stable, more satisfying, with a new quality of life less dependent on the emotional highs they looked for in their previous union. That is resurrection.

Scott is a public and professional person who finds his work sufficiently rewarding. But increasingly his success fails to provide an adequate degree of personal fulfillment. He feels that his life is devoid of meaning. Then it comes to him that perhaps he has been limiting his sense of who he really is. (Such moments of awakening are often the beginnings of new life in the growth process.) Perhaps he has indulged in a false conviction that in his restricted life he would be safe and secure. He

---

*Resurrection happens in the ordinariness of family and home situations.*

---

finds himself looking for a way out of what appears to be a dead-end situation. It is then that Scott manages to find a broader base on which to establish his person. He begins to arrange his time and space with relationships that minister to others and enable him to become more of what he is. In the process of moving away from the self as an exclusive center, he finds a richer and more abundant life. That is resurrection.

Carol has been suffering from muscular dystrophy since early childhood. She is now fifty years old and is confined to a wheelchair in a nursing home. She is unable to talk, is barely able to dress herself, and her food intake is limited to liquids and soft food. Her severest handicap is her inability to speak. She communicates with a "talking chart" which includes words most commonly used in ordinary conversation. She also constructs sentences from an alphabet card and seems to delight in the finger pointing involved.

Until Carol's mother died seven years ago, she provided loving home care for Carol. At her mother's request I have done some looking after Carol in these years. I visit her twice a month, and we have become close friends. The enrichment we enjoy is mutual. Between the "talking chart" and some improved sign language communication, we manage to have a fruitful and often fun-filled dialogue. Carol is unable to make more than a few audible sounds. Among them is an infectious giggle.

Often when I come to her room on a Friday afternoon, I will find Carol still in bed and obviously depressed. At heart she is a fun person, but she needs someone to talk with her and to listen to her. She needs someone to break the chain of loneliness and to dispel the sense of meaninglessness in her life, a feeling which seems at times to overtake her. Human survival and growth are dependent on relationships that are loving and affirming. Real communication, verbal and other kinds, are an indispensable must. What I have learned in this sometimes difficult relationship is that Carol comes to life after a somewhat extended visit.

I try to spend an hour and a half to two hours with her at each visit. This is enough time to enter into some in-depth communication. At times we have even engaged in some rather profound biblical discussion based on her favorite Scripture passages. She finds this very fulfilling, and it satisfies her hunger for spiritual development. What she needs more than to receive a hurried priestly blessing is to be fed with a proclamation of the Word. This is not her privilege. It is her right.

Lately I have found it satisfying to see her more alive and tuned in to things when I come to the end of my visit. The light in her eyes, the smile on her face, and the final hug — these tell me that something has happened on this afternoon. That is resurrection.

Resurrection! It happens in all kinds of ways, and often we will not be aware of it until suddenly, like the disciples on the road to Emmaus, we find that our "eyes are opened."

There are chronically ill people who, after a continuing struggle with pain, have finally come to a moment of truth, to that moment of acceptance which brings them to a truer sense of their identity, far beyond the limited sense they had come to believe was possible in their lives. That is resurrection.

Artists and composers speak of the so-called blocks that at times leave them frustrated, as the muse seems temporarily to abandon them and to leave them empty-handed for their efforts. But then new creative energy suddenly bursts forth and, in Shakespeare's words, "imagination bodies forth the forms of things unknown." At such moments they reach new peaks of creative achievement. It is a raising from the dead. It is resurrection.

Finally, resurrection happens in the ordinariness of family and home situations. When that troubled teenager who has been wallowing in self-pity ("You **never** let me do anything **I** want to do"), who, for several years, has been wandering aimlessly in that twilight zone we call adolescence, finally gets some sense into his or her head, and communication even becomes possible — that, too, is resurrection. (A word of caution is in order here. As far as expecting the teens to clean up those "disaster areas" commonly known as their bedrooms, it might be wise to simply forget about it. Even resurrection has its limits!)

If we have eyes to see, we will make all kinds of resurrection discoveries in the lives of people around us. The addicts of our day — the alcoholics, the drug abusers, the overeaters, the cigarette smokers, the gamblers — so many of them go through a death experience which we call "hitting bottom" before they come to a blessed cure, for themselves and for society. That is resurrection.

Resurrection! It's still going on. It happened to Jesus twenty centuries ago. It transformed the disciples who encountered Him and sent them forth to "renew the face of the earth." It's touching us today, and there are evidences all around that, since the memorable unleashing of power on that first Easter morning, things are simply not the same in our world. Teilhard de Chardin put it well: "Something is afoot in the universe and it seems to be transformation."

The Easter Preface of the Mass seems to say the same thing: "The joy of the resurrection fills the world."

This is not to deny the presence and reality of evil in the world. The shadows on the earth are all too prominent. But the shadows, after all, are but evidences of the prevailing presence of the light. Because of **Easter** we have reason to believe:

> *That in the struggle between the good*
> *and the bad, the good is ultimately*
> *going to win out; that life and love*
> *is stronger than death; and that*
> *there is always hope because Jesus*
> *is risen, and with, through, and in*
> *Him we are risen people and Easter*
> *is always.*

# Evil Days
# and the Present Opportunity

August 1, 1988

This word of God came to me on Saint Paul's wavelength in my morning meditation today: Make "the most of the opportunity, because the days are evil" (Ephesians 5:16). Ordinarily I'm not a prophet of doom, who spots only the darkness and the shadows on the earth. But "the days are evil" struck me as having special pertinence to our time. I don't quite know what evils Paul has in mind here as he admonishes the Ephesian converts of his day. He does make earlier mention of cosmic forces, the so-called principalities and powers, which are still abroad in the world. Jesus, he reminds them and us, has already triumphed over every demonic domination in the universe; nonetheless, these cosmic forces are still a threatening influence against which we need to take a firm stand. Objectively, we are already redeemed, but subjectively, we still need to freely appropriate to ourselves the saving power of Jesus. In the reign of God there is no cheap grace. Salvation is both God's gift and our task.

The evil days of Paul's time are more than likely matched by the collective evil of our own day. For starters, there is today a pervasive hypocrisy which assumes a righteous posture in the face of intolerable wrongs: Outright lying is euphemistically referred to as *disinformation;* exorbitant government spending outlays are justified in the name of *national security;* abortive killing of the unborn is referred to simply as *removal of fetal tissue;* and military invasions are called *necessary incursions* in the pursuit of national defense. The widening gap between the rich and the poor, we are told, is a necessary consequence of the free play of forces in the marketplace, and a 5 percent to 7 percent unemployment rate is allowable in the interest of a so-called healthy and competitive national economy. We find that the richest nation in the world is still unwilling to provide shelter and affordable housing for thousands of its people who are homeless and on the streets. Health care for more than 30 percent of its population continues to be an unresolved issue. Add to these the polluting of our air and our water, the squandering of our forests and the erosion of our soil. These are sins against creation, and they compound the evil of the sins against God and God's people in whom the Lord's glory is meant to come fully alive.

Here's a quote that describes a segment of America that quite a few people either envy or would like to join:

> They're young and they're greedy. He wears a Rolex President watch with his Brooks Brothers suspenders. She, in her power suit and floppy bow ties, carries a Coach Metropolitan bag. We — even those of us who may be a bit yuppie ourselves — hate their guts. They have too much money and spend it too freely — on themselves.

This quote does not come from a televangelist, although it easily could. It comes from, of all places, the *Wall Street Journal,* which is itself an influential money-making newspaper. It's not that being greedy has now become passé but just that money has become tighter. Suddenly the conspicuous overconsumption fad which declared that "you can have it all," and, after all, "greed is good," has now become impossible for many young overachievers.

So long as we remain insensitive to this and many other kinds of institutional violence, so long as we fail to work for systemic change that will turn things around and make transparent the healing and reconciling love of our God, who has created the good earth with enough to go around and for all to share, we cannot call ourselves Christian. To be Christian is, above all, to be on the side of the poor — to work for "liberty and justice for all," as the Pledge of Allegiance states.

A wise man once said that for evil to triumph all that's necessary is that good people do nothing. Paul rightly charges us to make "the most of the opportunity, because the days are evil."

# Death of a Dear Friend

September 16, 1988

A reflection on the death of my dear friend, Eleanore Taraboi.

She died as she had lived — feisty, strong, loving life to the end. That she struggled almost to the end to continue to live was a testimony to her deep appreciation of the gift of life. Oh, how she wanted just a few more years. As the poet Dylan Thomas would put it, she did "not go gentle into that good night," because she felt so strongly she had more things to do. After caring lovingly for her husband Frank during his several years of severe illness just previous to her own, she felt, as I suppose most of us would, that she had a right to a little more time — to enjoy her grandchildren, to take time for her close friends (more than a few!), yes, and to do some volunteer work for others.

But ultimately she accepted her death — not enthusiastically, to be sure, but with a readiness coupled with some reluctance, even as Jesus did. She was, throughout her life, very much an incarnationalist; that is, she believed thoroughly in the "enfleshment" of Jesus in human history, in Jesus who became totally one of us and was like us in all things except sin (see Hebrews 4:15). The human Jesus attracted her, the one who walked in our shoes and stayed around long enough to understand our situation, to feel our hurts, to enjoy our joys, to experience fully what it means to live a human life and, in so doing, to ultimately redeem it.

She had a deep faith in the resurrection of Jesus, which is the cause of our resurrection. The paschal mystery, the dying and rising of Jesus into which all of us were brought in Baptism, was the focus of her life. Dying and rising, His and ours — this she understood as it was played out in her life and in the lives of all of us. The rhythm of life's ups and downs were clearly for her a celebration of that mystery.

Among her several **close** friends, I was privileged, I believe, to be her closest. She had been so supportive of me that I found her person, her counsel, her enthusiasm and her energy for building up the Good Shepherd community to be an indispensable ingredient in my life. I once sent her a Christmas card on which I wrote: "You are more than a friend to me. You are a **part of me.**" She treasured those words, and now that she is no longer with us they take on a new meaning.

I experience a great emptiness, a deep void now — precisely, I think, because that "part of me" which she was is now missing. Death is many things, not the least of which is a tearing-asunder of relationships. As I grieve over her loss, I dare not harbor any bitterness, for she was a treasured gift to me for some twenty years. For this I can only be humbly grateful. In some ways her friendship with me has been a foretaste of that definitive communion we all long and hope for in the heavenly city where God is all in all and where the assurance of Jesus that we are His friends will be fully realized.

Ellie will be back. Of this I am sure. She'll be back in an improved and a corrected edition of resurrected life. In the interim, may she rest in that peace which is the legacy of Jesus and which she so richly deserves.

# Prayer: Welcoming
# the Word Already Within Us

September 20, 1988

Brother Guigo, a Carthusian Prior, in his "The Ladder of Monks" speaks of four rungs of the ladder in his "prayer exercise." Just as physical exercise must be regular if it is to promote true health and physical well-being, so we must be diligent and faithful to spiritual exercise to sustain spiritual health. He suggests that monks and all who wish to grow spiritually can advance by way of four stages, which are like four rungs of a ladder lifting us from earth to heaven: reading, meditation, prayer, and contemplation.

**Reading** is the careful study of a Scripture passage, concentrating all one's powers on it. **Meditation** is an application of the mind to acquiring knowledge of some hidden truth, preferably a scriptural truth. Such truth is never on the surface. One must drown oneself in the passage to discover its true meaning. The **prayer** that follows constitutes a turning of the heart, the center of a person's whole being, to God in order to drive out evil and assimilate what is good. The last rung, **contemplation,** is by far the most important. In this exercise one learns to let go and, as much as possible, get out of the way so that one can be lifted up to God and somehow experience what the psalmist exclaims: "Taste and see how good the LORD is . . ." (Psalm 34:9).

It must be remembered that these four rungs of the ladder do not constitute a strict methodology of prayer. They are not a pat "how to," but, rather, a suggested formula in which the four steps can be a helpful process to take us from where we are to where we want to be. In fact, we can fall into a prayer pattern by mounting any one of the rungs separately. A simple passage attentively read will easily lead to the thinking process we call meditation. Meditation, in turn, will naturally coalesce into prayer, and prayer properly pursued will almost inevitably lead us to the top rung of contemplation. Given the needs and disposition of the moment, we should always feel free to use these steps as the Spirit moves us.

A word about meditation is in order — it will flow rather quickly from the selected reading. If, as is generally the case, the choice is a Scripture passage, there is a special power here that will easily generate meditation. The word of God, Jesus assures us, is "Spirit and life." Indeed, in Saint James' letter we are reminded that the word of God is already within us. It needs only to be welcomed as he tells us: "Humbly welcome the word that has taken root in you, with its power to save you" (James 1:21).

In other words, the word of God is not something out there apart from us. Because we are "christened" people by Baptism, the word of God is already rooted in our hearts. We need only to open ourselves to it and give it welcome so that its fertility may surface. Prayerfully reading the word of God on the printed pages of the Scriptures will stir up that word which is already rooted within us. It will have power, as James tells us, to save. Here again, as in the case of God's presence to us, it is a question of our becoming consciously **aware** of that word which is already there. We humbly receive it and allow it to take hold of us. When we do this, we will want also to accept the ringing challenge of Saint James: "Act on this word. If all you do is listen to it, you are deceiving yourselves" (James 1:22). It is a favorite theme of this outspoken author that we be "doers of the word and not hearers only" (James 1:22).

Genuine prayer will never leave us passive and inactive. It will make us restless and push us out to involvement and engagement. The word in us will want to become flesh. We are assured by Isaiah:

> So shall my word be
>     that goes forth from my mouth;
> It shall not return to me void....
>                         Isaiah 55:11

As we come closer to our center, Christ, and through Him to our Father, we will also be more inevitably drawn to our brothers and sisters who, with us, are children of that same heavenly Father. We are like the spokes of a wheel — the closer they come to their center, the closer they come to each other. We are like Saint Paul — the more he advanced in prayer, the more he experienced the Spirit urging him, pressing him on to ever greater apostolic works until he was able to exclaim: "I have worked harder than all the others..." (1 Corinthians 15:10). Yet, he was quick to add that it was not he who was working but Christ who lived in him. For Paul and for us, prayer must be the soul of the apostolate. Our external works will always be measured by the quality of our interior life. "You will know them by their deeds" (Matthew 7:16).

Traditionally, prayer falls into four categories: praise, thanksgiving, repentance, and petition. The first three are quite understandable. Because God is who God is — our Creator on whom we are totally dependent, as well as our Savior who has come to our rescue — it is absolutely appropriate that as creatures we acknowledge this dependence by our praise and adoration. Not that God needs our praise, but at the deepest source of our being we need to praise God. Which is to say, we need to shout *hallelujah* so that others will hear and know what God has done and is doing for us.

Likewise, thanking God is understandably appropriate because God is our benefactor, and we are the beneficiaries. Even more obvious is our common need to seek forgiveness from what we know to be an all-forgiving God.

When we come to petition, or intercessory prayer, however, things become somewhat problematic because here we enter into the realm of profound mystery. And yet for many people this is probably the only prayer they have learned to pray. Because they are so totally dependent on God, they turn to

---

*Does something really happen when we petition God or when we pray for others, living or dead?*

---

God instinctively in their many needs. Invariably when you talk to people about prayer you find that they understand prayer in terms largely of what they pray for. But clearly there are nagging questions that need to be asked here.

Does something really happen when we petition God or when we pray for others, living or dead? After all, doesn't God care for others' needs far more than we do? Also, do we need to clue God in on those needs? Do we refresh God's memory? And what about our free will if God intervenes? These are questions not easily answered.

One thing comes to mind to shed a bit of light on this puzzling prayer problem. When we petition God, for ourselves or for others, we are obviously expressing our dependence on

God and our need of God. This is worship — the creature acknowledging the Creator. The relationship between the child and the Parent is being properly recognized.

Mystery aside, however, Jesus does expect us to pray in this way. In Matthew's text we have the obvious parallel between a human father and the heavenly Father and the contract: "If you, with all your sins, know how to give your children what is good, how much more will your heavenly Father give good things to anyone who asks . . . !" (Matthew 7:11). The how-much-more argument becomes even more forceful in Luke, who, after using Matthew's identical words in the first portion of the question, concludes then with this provocative addition: " . . . how much more will the heavenly Father give the holy Spirit to those who ask . . ." (Luke 11:13). Luke, moreover, insists that we ask, knock, and seek on a continuing basis (Luke 11:9). What he really means is that we keep on asking, keep on knocking, and keep on seeking, and our petitions will invariably be answered with the best possible "good thing," the Holy Spirit. In this sense, no prayer ever goes unanswered, for, unfailingly, God will give us what we most need, namely the Spirit — the Spirit who alone can transform us and lead us into God's reign. When we have the Spirit, we have it all. When we have the Spirit, we have run out of all needs. It is clear that in all our prayer God's arm is never going to be twisted. God's plan is never changed. What does happen is that we are changed and brought in sync with the overarching plan of God.

**FIRE**

# The Meaning of Celibacy

November 9, 1988

Just returned from our monthly Lutheran-Episcopal-Catholic clergy dialogue at Our Savior's Lutheran Church in Milwaukee. Our topic: *celibacy.* For centuries the Church has made the celibate life a requirement for priestly ordination. For the priest, there were no options. One had to accept this whole package of total commitment — of all or nothing — in the choice of the ministry.

Why celibacy? What does it mean to be celibate? What statement does it make to the world outside? It certainly signifies much more than the discipline required for abstention from genital activity. Celibacy surely does not intend to demean the sacredness of sexual expression in the practice of conjugal love. Nor does it declare that the married state is inferior in any way to the celibate vocation because in either case we are talking about sacred covenant relationships between persons — in the case of marriage, between husband and wife, and in celibacy, between the celibate and the Lord — a covenant that reflects the psalmist's words: "God is the rock of my heart and my portion forever" (Psalm 73:26). The celibate means to say, "To God alone do I give my life and my total self."

In much the same way do husband and wife in a Christian sacramental marriage give themselves to each other in a love relationship which mirrors and participates in the covenantal union between God and God's people. In the New Testament it is between Christ and His bride, the Church. Both are sacred unions and calls to holiness, equal but different.

Question: Is this what celibacy actually continues to **say** to people in today's world? In a culture and society which today is so sex-driven, does celibacy appear to be a totally incomprehensible and irrelevant choice? Does the celibate person give witness, as he or she is called to do, to a totally committed life in the service of God's people? Is he or she truly a sign of that unique and eschatological love which Jesus points to in the kingdom of God? A kingdom which is already here but not yet fully — where there is a transcendent love which is total and unconditional and which all of us are ultimately called to in the heavenly city?

There was general agreement in our discussion that the celibate sign must be more than exterior. It must be an outward sign that is inwardly fulfilled. It must be given a genuine form that clearly bears witness in each concrete historical situation. The sign must speak in this person, in this celibate man or woman — that there is at least a spark of that flame of love which the world has come to see in Christ Jesus. There is no room in such a life for substitutes to compensate for the spiritual discipline associated with sexual abstinence — no room for a life sated with lust for power, with an addiction to luxury, or with resentment against life. The celibate, like anyone else, must come to healthy terms with his or her sexuality and integrate it into his or her committed life. Any kind of prudery can only blur the witness that the celibate is called to give.

Needless to say, the celibate priest is going to find that roughly one half of the people in his congregation are going to be women. He cannot afford to be uncomfortable in his pastoral relationships with women and so risk alienating a sizable number of his parishioners. Sexism of any kind is hardly excusable, much less at a time when the women's rights movement is in the forefront. It becomes even more intolerable when viewed in the New Testament perspective. The Gospels clearly portray Jesus as showing considerable preference for marginalized people, including women. His dealings with the woman taken in adultery and the Samaritan woman are striking examples of his determination to violate existing taboos which continued to treat women as inferior members of God's people.

An interesting sidelight here. I was asked by the clergy in our dialogue (presumably because I was the oldest surviving celi-

---

*. . . no one escapes the pain of loneliness.*

---

bate present in the group!) how I managed after more than fifty years of celibate "abstention" to retain some semblance of being a normal member of the male species. I explained how in my seminary training we were given almost no credible spirituality to support the celibacy requirement. By implication, however unintentional this was on the part of our instructors at the time, it seemed to us that sexual expression had no place in the confines of the sacred and that somehow women in particular were a source of danger to the spiritual life of the priest. (We were told, when driving our cars, to relegate women to the back seat!)

However, in spite of this suspicious negativism in regard to the "weaker sex," which might have colored in some way my earlier years in the priesthood, I did succeed in ministering fairly successfully to all people, and even, I think, especially to women. My family background was helpful, because my mother and sisters always appeared to me to be less than a "dangerous species." And, when in the late '40s I became deeply involved in the Christian Family Movement, I found that the many hours I spent in family settings in couples' homes, in preparing and attending meetings — with the couples' children often interrupting and seeking their attention — enabled me more and more to integrate my single and celibate life with the gritty and down-to-earth realities of ordinary people and their daily lives. I truly believe they did more for me than I ever did for them.

We talked a bit about the inevitable aloneness which is part of celibate living — aloneness which often leads to loneliness. After a busy day in ministering to others, the celibate priest comes to his empty room. There is no one there. No one to share his day's experiences, his pains and his joys, his highs and his lows. Our discussion ended in a conclusion based on common human experience: No one escapes the pain of aloneness.

Married people who are in well-adjusted marriages and who communicate regularly will confess to times when they feel utterly alone, when they are unable somehow to share those mysterious voids that are lodged in the deep recesses of the human psyche. Some hungers and expectations are destined never to be revealed or satisfied. Perhaps this is because each human person participates in some way in the mystery of that God in whose image and likeness he or she is created. Or is it the Creator's way of saying that we cannot have it **all** in the here-and-now? We live with human limitations. Saint Augustine says it well: "Thou hast made us for thyself, O God, and our hearts are restless until they find their rest in Thee."

# God's Turn

February 8, 1989

It's Ash Wednesday and once again we are called to make that annual retreat — the journey "from ashes to Easter." I'm still haunted by some of those Lents of old when we were obsessed with giving up things. My recollection is that we gave up very little but somehow the minimal suffering made us feel less guilty.

Giving up something can easily serve to feed one's ego and relieve some of the inner anxiety caused by the sinfulness that is so much a part of our human equipment. But it is hardly the purpose of Lent to free us from our anxiety closets. So it seems to me we had better start our Lenten journey by giving up "giving up" and getting on with the real business of this time of healing, which is to change our hearts. Thomas Merton warns us against exaggerating our tiny sacrifices by making them seem either unbearable or else more heroic than they actually are. Such sacrifice, he tells us, would be better left unmade. "Better to eat a dinner in full gratitude," he cautions us, "than to make some picayune sacrifice of part of it, with the feeling that one is suffering martyrdom." Done without love, sacrifices can only be self-serving. They are never redemptive.

The key word to a true Lenten observance is *turn*. In the first reading from Ash Wednesday's Mass, the prophet Joel cries out the Lord's words:

> Yet even now . . .
> return to me with your whole heart. . . .
>
> Joel 2:12

Fasting, almsgiving, and prayer are the traditional outward signs of this turning. But the prophet quickly reminds us that the essential turning is inward.

> Rend your hearts, not your garments. . . .
>
> Joel 2:13

Our own turning to the Lord will trigger the Lord's turning to us, for the Lord is

> . . . gracious and merciful . . .
> slow to anger, rich in kindness. . . .
>
> Joel 2:13

It is clear that God's turning to us is way out of proportion to the minimal turning we render to God. Our "rent" hearts, our prayer and fasting, our sacrifices are countered by God's gift of life. In Jesus, God has turned to take our flesh so that we in turn might share God's divine nature. Jesus became "sin" for us, as Saint Paul puts it, so that we might become "the very holiness of God" (2 Corinthians 5:21).

Karl Rahner recalls in unforgettable words that in Jesus "God has irrevocably turned his face to us in love." As a consequence we are a new creation, ambassadors for Christ in the great redemptive work of reconciliation. The purpose of Lent is none other than to fix our gaze intently on this Jesus in whom the Father has turned to us that we might turn to each other and all together return to God.

# The Many Temptations of Christ

February 11, 1989

I haven't seen *The Last Temptation of Christ,* so I will not venture to critique the film. But some of the fuss and furor I've been hearing about it makes me suspect that perhaps this movie isn't all that bad. Most of the outrage is at the thought of Jesus being tempted sexually, even though He never in any way succumbs to the temptation.

Apparently there are many folks who cannot accept a Jesus who is totally human. They'll accept Him being human all right, but not **that** human. But pure logic suggests that if He is truly human and like us in all things except sin (see Hebrews 4:15), then He had to accept the whole human package, including being liable to temptations of a sexual nature.

I personally am more comfortable with a tempted Christ who joined us in all our struggles than with a Christ exempt from carrying some of our baggage. He would, in fact, be someone less than human, or indeed not human at all. Would we not be doing Him and the Creator God a disservice to deny His humanness in all its dimensions? In so doing, would we not blur the reality of God's liberating love in identifying the divine self unequivocally with our human situation in the great plan of the incarnation?

We desperately need a God who has stood in our shoes and experienced the total range of possibilities as we trudge our way on the human journey. We are told ". . . the Word became flesh" (John 1:14), and that means our flesh with all its vulnerability as well as its possibilities. We feel much better about the precious gift of our sexuality as we contemplate Jesus having to cope with the reality of the day-to-day temptations that are often associated with this powerful and sometimes explosive God-given human drive.

The Gospel of this first Sunday of Lent puts the focus of Jesus' temptation where it squarely belongs — namely, on His mission as a messiah, on total obedience and acceptance of that mission wherever it might lead. In fact, it would result, as He later discovered, in

> . . . becoming obedient to death,
> even death on a cross.
> Philippians 2:8

for us and for all humankind.

Whatever the gravity of His sexual temptations, it is clear from the Gospel that these are not central to what He was called upon to resist in life. It was rather the temptation to be some other kind of messiah than what the Father was calling Him to be. To turn stone into bread, to throw Himself down from the turret of the temple, and to embrace the kingdoms of the world by bowing down to Satan (see Matthew 4:1-11) would have been, in other words, to become self-serving and to put faith in other things, in power, and in the use of the spectacular in order to win approval for His saving mission. His was a temptation ultimately to harbor despair, to refuse to trust totally and absolutely in a God who would be with Him and for Him even when all seemed doomed to failure and frustration. This temptation was destined to be with Him to the end, even when He was dying on the cross, as is evident from His cry: "My God, my God, why have you forsaken me?" (Matthew 27:46). And it was this temptation, so palpably more difficult to resist than any sexual allurement, that Jesus finally and unmistakably was able to overcome: "Father, into your hands I commend my spirit" (Luke 23:46). For Him this had to be the last word. So is it also for us!

# Letting the Poor into Our Lives

April 14, 1989

*Preferential option for the poor!* It has become a much-used expression in the Church today, a kind of buzz phrase frequently found in Church documents, encyclicals, and theological journals. It's a concept that has a long history in our Christian Church, but the phrase is of recent origin — used especially by the South American bishops and by liberation theologians. Pope John Paul II and the United States bishops have also used it.

What does the phrase mean? Very simply, it means that as Christians we need to have a frame of mind, a perspective, or an attitude in which the poor are never excluded. It means that we position ourselves unmistakably on the side of the poor because they are powerless and have no one to speak for them. *Preferential* suggests that the poor and their needs are given preference as opposed to a grudging tolerance. *Option* means taking a stand on behalf of the poor and choosing to walk with them in their struggle. In their pastoral on the economy, the bishops conclude that a nation's economy must be judged precisely on what it does **for** poor people and **to** poor people — and what it enables poor people to do for themselves.

This whole notion is very controversial and raises many eyebrows in our country. It's a truly radical imperative suggesting that in the transformation of society, the poor must be given first consideration. Excluded from enjoying the blessings of the American dream, they presently are left on the fringe of society. Catholic social teaching considers this an affront to their human dignity in reducing them to being noncontributing members of an economic system that puts a high priority on teamwork and full collaboration. As such, poor people produce little and consume less. From a purely economic standpoint, they contribute almost nothing to the so-called bottom line.

But from an ethical perspective, the presence of poor people in significant numbers is a serious judgment on our system. Thirty-five percent of United States people fall below the poverty line and another 15 percent just above that level. Pope John Paul insists that worldwide, the widening gap between the rich and the poor is not pure accident. We have poor people, he tells us, because we have structured our society to create poor people and to keep them poor. It doesn't have to be that way, he assures us, and the situation is not simply the consequence of blind economic forces at work. Because we tolerate poverty and allow it to happen, we have **decided for it** and we are morally remiss. We are guilty of what he calls *structured sin.* Institutional evil, some call it.

The Gospel and Church documents require us, as Christians, to be advocates for the poor. This includes rejecting some of the common myths about the poor:

(a) "The poor you will always have with you," we are told. Jesus did indeed say this (see Matthew 26:11), but not to condone the situation. He was merely stating an empirical fact.

(b) "The poor are happy. They like it that way." The homeless, it is said, choose to be on the streets.

Studies, however, show that the poor by and large do not like being poor.

(c) "Poverty is relative. We are all poor in some way," people say. But this blurs the reality.

It is sad that there is a growing punitive attitude toward the poor. Some persons suggest that if we stop "coddling the poor" and punish them enough, they will somehow stop being poor. Experience shows that it doesn't work that way. Opposing this view is Jesus who calls the poor

"Blessed . . .
for theirs is the kingdom of heaven."
Matthew 5:3

He Himself was born in poverty and lived as a poor man who had "nowhere to lay his head" (Luke 9:58). He was poor in the total sense and calls on us to imitate Him who emptied Himself to be with us and for us. He ate with the poor and, because they were powerless, He became their advocate and preferentially sided with them.

In parables Jesus warned against accumulating riches. "Look at the birds in the sky; they do not sow or reap . . . yet your heavenly Father feeds them" (Matthew 6:26). The lust for wealth diminishes our trust in a providing God, He seemed to say. To inquiring disciples of John the Baptist, He said, "Go and tell John what you hear and see: the blind regain their sight, the lame walk, lepers are cleansed, the deaf hear, the dead are raised, and the poor have the good news proclaimed to them" (Matthew 11:4-5). He commanded His disciples to travel light in their ministry. Finally, in a most devastating way He specifically identified Himself, His own person, with the poor when He declared " . . . whatever you did for one of these least . . . you did for me" (Matthew 25:40). In rejecting the poor, His "least," we are rejecting Him.

This hard teaching is clearly countercultural in a nation

where the gospel of "help yourself" and "lift yourself up by your own bootstraps" is widely preached and practiced. Not to make it in our competitive society is a sure sign that we are lazy, shiftless freeloaders. It leaves no margin for the structured, institutional evil which leaves many to sink into poverty. An obvious example: Congress and the President are presently in a hassle about raising the current minimum wage by a sum of somewhere between 90 cents and $1.25 an hour. In spite of a 40 percent inflationary increase in the cost of living since 1980, our working poor are still earning at that subminimum

---

*Christian stewardship should call us to take a good look at our life-style. . . .*

---

level of $3.35 an hour. Such haggling for a few dimes for the poor is a glaring example of structured evil.

What to do? Direct aid to feed and generally help the poor is a minimum requirement for all of us. It provides a necessary Band-Aid to afford immediate assistance to the poor. But it dare not stop there. Justice demands that we seriously set about the task of changing a system which continues to breed poverty. Whatever I can do to transform society, to bring about systemic or institutional change — by the votes I cast in selecting public officials, by the money I spend on impulse buying, by the way I invest my money so that the poor will not be further oppressed, by the way I teach my children — these are but some of the things I, as a Christian, can do to reverse some of the wrongs perpetrated in our time against society's underclass.

Having a preferential option for the poor does not mean that we reject the nonpoor or wish to generate class hatred, and it does not mean that we intend to romanticize the poor, who are not always in the category of the innocent. Original sin, after all, is pretty well spread all around. But it does mean that we have a feeling for the poor, that we are touched by their situation and experience hurt when we see the spectacle of hunger and homelessness, when we see the bloated bellies and sunken eyes of malnourished children on our television screens.

Christian stewardship should call us to take a good look at our life-style, to sort out in our consuming habits the difference between indispensable, necessary things and things that are merely convenient or superfluous. There are admirable examples of people who volunteer to tithe their time to transform society. In this way they are indirectly letting people into their lives. To do nothing is to allow evil to prevail. It is to commit the sin of omission.

If we don't let the poor into our lives, we miss a chance to meet Jesus!

**FIRE**

# The Rich Person's Problem

May 12, 1989

About the danger of riches as described in the Gospel of Luke — Jesus comes back to it time and time again. He doesn't condemn wealth as such, but assures us that it is very difficult for the rich person to enter the kingdom of God. (Easier for the camel to pass through the eye of a needle, He reminds us, than for the rich man to enter heaven.) We feel impelled to say to Jesus, "Why do you keep repeating this? We've heard it again and again." And we can almost hear Him reply, "Yes, that's just the problem. You have heard it but what are you doing about it?"

In Saint James' letter we are reminded that our call is to be "doers of the word and not hearers only" (James 1:22). In the parable of the rich man and Lazarus, we have an example of the striking gap that separates the rich from the poor. The rich man, dressed in fine garments, is dining sumptuously day after day with wealthy friends at his table. And just a few hundred yards away at his gates sits the poor man Lazarus waiting and hoping for some leftover crumbs that might fall from that table. But they never come. Then, one day the rich man dies and goes into the abode of the abyss, an Old Testament metaphor for eternal punishment or hell. And the poor man dies and resides in the bosom of Abraham. The rich man is cursed; the poor man enjoys blessing (see Luke 16:19-31).

An interesting note in this parable is the total lack of any confrontation between the rich man and Lazarus. We don't see Lazarus knocking at the rich man's door, pleading with him and reaching out for some bits of food. And we don't have the rich man rejecting him outright, telling him to get off his premises, to stop being so shiftless and lazy, telling him he must learn to help himself and lift himself up by his own bootstraps. None of this. The rich man has a problem, but it isn't that he is spiteful or hateful. It isn't simply that he possesses riches. His problem is — he doesn't care. It isn't as if the poor man Lazarus were miles away and out of sight, living in some inner-city slum. Not out there in Lebanon somewhere. Lazarus is right here within eyeshot of the rich man, who doesn't move a finger. His sin is a sin of omission. He doesn't care!

What identifies Jesus most clearly in the Gospels is that He cares. He shows a distinct preference for lepers, poor people, widows, the sick, and outcasts; in a word, the vulnerable people, the little ones who have no clout and no one to speak for them. The people who have nothing to say and perhaps wouldn't know how to say it if they did. These are the people who tear at Jesus' heart and move Him to compassion. He feeds the hungry multitude, touches the bier of the widow's son at Naim and restores him to life. He goes to the tomb of Lazarus at the bidding of Mary and Martha and brings him back to life. Jesus shows a special concern for sinners, for publicans known to be corrupt. In His dying moments on the cross when He might legitimately be tempted to think of His own needs and to look for some compassion from others, He prays for his enemies: "Father, forgive them, they know not what they do" (Luke 23:34). He prays for the thief on the right who pleads for a merciful remembrance. " . . . today," he says, "you will be with me in Paradise" (Luke 23:43).

The essential mark of a disciple of Jesus is to be a caring person. The very end of Matthew's Gospel is punctuated with that famous last judgment scene where the measure of whether we are to be received into His kingdom, to be the sheep on His right or the goats on His left, is determined by how much we cared: "I was hungry, I was thirsty, I was in prison, you fed me, you gave me something to drink, you visited me. I was hungry, you did not give me anything to eat; I was thirsty, you did not give me anything to drink; I was in prison, you did not visit me. As often as you did it to one of these least brothers and sisters of mine, you did it to me" (see Matthew 25:31-46).

To love God and especially to love God in the neighbor: that's the core of the Gospel demand. The possession of wealth is not Jesus' primary concern. It is how we use our wealth that concerns Him. He has no tolerance for those who simply don't care. Our final judgment may likely be not so much on what we have done but on what we haven't done.

# The Blood of Martyrs

July 4, 1989

Shen Tong, a Chinese student active in the recent pro-democracy movement which ended so tragically when army troops bore down with tanks and guns on the demonstrators, safely escaped China and landed in this country on June 11. Now studying biology at Brandeis University, this courageous student, who is being sought by Chinese authorities, has broken a self-imposed silence in a press interview. What this lanky self-assured fugitive has to say is worth listening to.

To Shen Tong, the experience was a "grand-scale self-education of what democracy really is" and, because "the seeds of democracy have been sown," he now vows to carry on democratic reforms in exile. There is considerable evidence that many students and Chinese people have the courage of their convictions to continue the struggle for radical change in China.

You can quell an uprising in the short run, especially if you have the army to impose your will, but in the long run you cannot kill rising expectations that have their roots in an idea so true it simply will not die. It is the Chinese people's hope (and ours) that this first encounter in the struggle for participatory government — and what Shen Tong calls a "complete victory" — will come to an early and full fruition.

On this Fourth of July we cannot help comparing the extraordinary courage of these thousands of Chinese people, who dared to stand their ground in the face of appalling odds in Tiananmen Square on June 4, to the bravery of our own historic freedom fighters in 1776, who pledged to lay down their very lives for an idea that has revolutionalized the world. History will not fail to record that in each instance the blood-letting that at the time seemed so senseless and unnecessary was, in the end, redemptive. The blood of these martyrs was not shed in vain, for with it the seeds of democracy were sown.

# The God Who Suffers

July 4, 1989

A reflection on the Passion narrative according to Saint Matthew: A God who suffers becomes a profound mystery. We regard suffering as a specifically human limitation. Yet the Jewish Talmud assures us that God indeed suffers with us. God joins us on our human journey; God understands our pain. Our Lord chooses to share the ambiguities of our human situation. And in Jesus, God has opted to go all the way in becoming enfleshed in our humanity. Jesus sheds our tears, sweats our blood, and dies our death. He experiences firsthand our living, suffering, and dying. His cry from the cross — "My God, my God, why have you forsaken me?" (Mark 15:34) — echoes the cry of desolation that goes out from all humanity throughout human history.

We feel compelled to ask: Why did Jesus choose to suffer? To hurt with our hurts, to know our loneliness and depression even to the extent of accepting our death? We can only presume that He wanted to understand better what it means to be human. An old Indian saying has it that you don't really know a person until you stand in that person's moccasins and walk around awhile. But it is even more likely that in His unconditional acceptance of our humanness Jesus wanted us to understand better the full extent of God's love for us.

The image of Jesus with His tortured body stretched out on the cross as if to embrace the whole world provides an unmistakable sign of God's incomparable love. The message could hardly be missed. In John's words, "For God so loved the world that he gave his only Son" (John 3:16). And the Son so loved us that He gave Himself for our salvation.

Jesus not only suffers with us, He also suffers for us. He assumes our burden and our guilt and so bridges the gulf caused by our sin. The suffering and death of Jesus is a reconciling and redemptive act. "For he is our peace," Paul reminds us (Ephesians 2:14). In the stations of the cross, we used to pray at each station, "We adore You, O Christ, and we bless You, because by Your holy cross You have redeemed the world."

In one of his many remarkable stories, Elie Wiesel, the famous Jewish novelist, has one of his characters, Yehuda, mildly rebuke his dear friend Gregor, who is going through a painful depression in his life. Yehuda is concerned because Gregor is turning in on himself, isolating himself in his suffering. Yehuda tries to persuade him, rather, to open himself to others in his ordeal. Otherwise, he is merely shriveling himself.

It is clear that Jesus in His suffering does not isolate Himself from us. His outstretched arms on the cross are a sign of openness to the world He is redeeming and are an invitation to us to open ourselves to others in our pain. He tells us that our suffering, too, can be redemptive. If we turn inward in a spirit of self-pity, our suffering becomes a waste. When we, as Christians, join our pain to Christ's, we can in some way have an impact on the universe. We build up the body of Christ. Saint Paul assures us: "I have been crucified with Christ" (Galatians 2:19). In another mysterious passage he reminds us that when we suffer in union with Jesus we are somehow "filling up what is lacking in the afflictions of Christ on behalf of his body, which is the church" (Colossians 1:24). Somehow we can help complete what is seemingly incomplete. Jesus, if you will, makes necessary our pain joined to His in order to bring to completion the redemptive pool of suffering.

Finally, what was truly unique about the suffering of Jesus was that He suffered with love. Without love, suffering has no meaning. Suffering with love is sacrifice and becomes redeeming. The death of Jesus, then, is more than sheer crucifixion. It is crucified love which alone saves the world, transforms us, reconciles us to God, making it possible for us to be one with Him in faith, hope, and love. As Christians, we are called to come after Jesus, to imitate that crucified love, and in some way to make that love of Jesus transparent in our lives.

# The Nonviolence of God

September 12, 1989

I've been thinking a lot about nonviolence lately. The older I get, the more I am drawn to a nonviolent stance, not only as an anti-war position, but, more important, as a way of life.

In the '60s the nation was shocked by the assassinations of President John F. Kennedy, his brother Bobby, and Martin Luther King. There were many thoughtful people then who concluded that we are essentially a violent society. Much has happened in the years since to corroborate that assessment. The news headlines and TV newscasts provide daily instances of killings in our neighborhoods, of muggings on our streets, of tavern brawls, of drug and gang-war retaliations, of rape, of wife-beating and child abuse, of robberies and theft — and this is only some of the clear evidence of a violent society.

On the global scene there is violence on a much more gigantic scale as wars of one kind or another continue in more than a dozen trouble spots around the world. Add to this the plundering of our environment the world over — the polluting of our air and water, the scandalous raping of our soil and natural resources — and you have a quantum of wholesale aggression that is a shameful affront on the sacredness of persons and things.

History reveals that there are three ways of resolving disputes in human relationships:

(a) Retaliation or revenge is one way. In the Old Testament there was no recourse to justice other than to apply the law of "getting even" in order to make things equal. Getting even was also a way to prevent the other from doing even greater harm. It was a beginner's law, the law of retaliation — "eye for eye, tooth for tooth" (Exodus 21:24; see also Matthew 5:38).

(b) In the New Testament the principle, "Do to others whatever you would have them do to you" (Matthew 7:12), becomes a less harsh way of resolving disputes. Because we'd like others to treat us even better than we would expect, it represents an advance, going a step further in the resolution of conflict.

(c) The way of nonviolence is the third way. This is God's way. God is nonviolent. God is contemplative — which is to say, God has total self-knowledge. Our Creator knows a oneness with each one of us and with all creation. We are all distinct from, but never separate from, our Creator. God is constantly present to all that is created, and all that is created God loves unconditionally. Because we are so intimately a part of God and made to the divine image and likeness, God has no choice but to love. God can never turn against God's handiwork. In Jesus' words, the Lord makes the sun "rise on the bad and the good" (Matthew 5:45). The Lord's love for us does not depend on what we say or do.

If, in turn, we know totally who we are, one with and part of God as well as one with one another, then we, too, will be nonviolent. Then, not only the remotest stranger whom we have never seen, not only the enemy who hates us, but also all those we do see will be seen as brothers and sisters whom we dare not violate. They will be seen as brothers and sisters whom we have no choice but to love because, as the title of a book by Louis Evely states, *That Man Is You.* No rational person hates himself or herself.

In the Gospel Jesus invites us to learn from Him because He is meek (see Matthew 11:29). This is a call to a nonviolence that refuses to strike back and even the score. In every instance when Jesus was violated, He refused to retaliate. He stopped the flow of violence. He rebuked Peter for cutting off the soldier's ear in the Garden of Gethsemane, reminding him that those who live by the sword will perish by the sword. Instead of striking back at the servant of the high priest who struck Him in the face, He simply rebuked him with mild words of fraternal correction: ". . . if I spoke the truth, why hit me?" (John 18:23). His prayer for His enemies in His dying moments on the cross constitutes history's most unforgettable expression of nonviolent and forgiving love: "Father, forgive them, they know not what they do" (Luke 23:34).

Lest anyone charge that the nonviolence of Jesus is a sign of weakness that only permits evil to prevail and escalate, a more careful reading of the Gospels will show that Jesus was neither wimpy nor weak, allowing others to do just as they wanted to Him. He resisted the scribes and the Pharisees for their hypocrisy and oppression of the poor by denouncing the evil with a nonviolent response. His angry outburst when He overthrew the tables of the money-changers, whose trafficking and marketing in the temple violated the sacredness of God's house, was an act of nonviolent resistance. He could not tolerate the desecration of that holy place in Jerusalem, which was so unmistakably a sign of the presence of God among the people. More than anything, He wanted it to be a teaching moment:

> "My house shall be a house of prayer,
> but you are making it a den of thieves."
>> Matthew 21:13

Because Jesus believed that truth has an inherent power to free people and to bring about change, He chose to confront people with the truth rather than to attack them. He knew that truth could have an effect even on a so-called adversary. He wanted to discover the hidden truth that can be found even in that person who appeared to be an enemy but who was, in truth, a brother or sister. Father William Shannon, in his book, *Seeking the Face of God,* puts this whole concept best when he says, "Jesus refused to allow people to make him hate them."

For more than three hundred years the first Christians lived by the principle of nonviolence. Jesus and His message were understood by them to be countercultural. As disciples, they had no alternative but to imitate and witness to His Spirit. They chose not to enter the military. War as a means of resolving conflict was considered intolerable and wrong. The so-called Just War Theory began to be upheld only after Constantine the Great (A.D. 275-337) ruled the Roman Empire, and the early Christians began increasingly to accept and assimilate the secular culture. It was an unhappy compromise that often allowed the Church to at least condone and even to participate in countless wars for more than fifteen hundred years. The right to defend oneself against an unjust aggressor was grounded on a Greek philosophical rationale which, unfortunately, had no foundation in the Gospel.

Strangely, this principle of justifiable self-defense was not questioned by individuals or nations until the last few decades when it was challenged by such champions as Gandhi, Dorothy Day, and a few pacifist groups who were considered impractical idealists. In all of these wars, in Thomas Merton's words, "God was the first to be enlisted." All combatants invariably counted the Divinity on their side in what was presumably a righteous cause. In World War II neither the indiscriminate fire-bombing of entire cities and the mass killings of thousands of innocent civilians, nor even the horrible slaughter of more than 70,000 Japanese noncombatants from the dropping of the hydrogen bomb on Hiroshima, succeeded in causing more than a minimal stirring of the world conscience.

Today, however, there is a growing awareness that war as an instrument of resolving conflict has become completely outmoded. The nuclear bomb has made fighting anything approximating a war directed at limited targets practically impossible. The nuclear arms race and the cold war have not only depleted the earth's resources at an enormous rate, but threaten at the same time to destroy all life as we have come to know it on our Planet Earth. As a result, war has become morally indefensible, and continuance of the arms race in the face of the urgent needs of millions of our people has become an international scandal. Even military experts hold that modern warfare can

---

*I am most like Him when I respect the dignity of every human person as inviolate . . .*

---

produce nothing but losers. Nothing short of an all-out peace effort will now make sense. Even the mere possession of these weapon stockpiles as a so-called deterrent in the interest of defense is being seriously questioned as a moral option because of the ever-present temptation of a first-strike usage.

We need to heed the words of Pope Paul VI: "No more war! Never again war!"

The Lord, speaking to the Israelites of old, put before them the choice of life or death and then urged them, "Choose life" (Deuteronomy 30:19). Today we have but one choice — to choose life. The United States bishops in their famous peace pastoral, issued seven years ago, seemed to indicate that the unfolding of today's events is driving us to peace because there is no viable alternative. History, they tell us, is providentially offering us "a new moment" — the beginning of the nuclear age, which they view as a moment of decision. Either we will choose a **demonic** moment of courting the danger of a nuclear holocaust or a **creative** moment of ordering our world in a way that relegates war to the past of human history.

If a "just war" is no longer an acceptable option in the way nations deal with each other in their global disputes, then, for me, the choice of observing a nonviolent posture in all my interpersonal relationships should be a next logical step. From this day forward I want this to be the "new moment" in my life. Jesus is the nonviolence of God made visible among us. I am most like Him when I respect the dignity of every human person as inviolate — that is, when I refuse to be the bearer of violence. This is none other than the challenge of Jesus who calls us to be perfect as our heavenly Father is perfect (see Matthew 5:48).

Concretely, this means that every time I put someone down, diminish a person with a cutting remark, speak the careless word that inflicts pain — I am being a violent person. Every time I make fun of another, to that person's face privately or in public — I am being a violent person and I have shut off the current of healing love that flows from what Saint Paul calls "the power of his [Jesus'] resurrection" (Philippians 3:10).

Presently I am miles from reaching this ideal, but from this moment on I want nonviolence to be the goal toward which my life in Christ is moving.

# Believers and Doers

October 18, 1989

A contemporary sociologist, Gordon Allport, completed a recent survey of so-called religious people. His study concluded that the more "religious" people are, the more prejudiced, racist, and bigoted they tend to be.

He divided the people into two classes. The first group were those who externalized their religion, equating religion with prayer, worship, church attendance, regulations, and ritual. They wanted preaching that would comfort them and bring them peace. They objected to homilies that touched on controversial or political topics. They wanted a biblical word that was reassuring rather than challenging. They didn't think the pulpit was a place to make waves. The second group were those who felt they were called to be the salt of the earth and the light of the world. They preferred a religion that focused on activism. They believed in the importance of ritual but were never squeamish about missing Sunday worship. More important, they felt a need to be prophetic, to live lives that would make an impact on the world and make a difference.

What is urgently needed in the Church today is to get these two crowds together — the worshipers and activists, the believers and the doers. We need people who will be willing to go up to the temple to pray, and then to go forth from the temple to the world outside and make their presence felt.

Authentic religion will always project a faith that shows that the altar and the pulpit are truly related to the marketplace and society — a faith which, in Archbishop Rembert Weakland's words, "is also a sign that we want to be a part of what is happening in that society."

# Ecumenism:
# We Are Already One

January 25, 1990

Today ends the annual Octave of Prayer for Christian Unity. One of the key theological statements in the Vatican II *Decree on Ecumenism* assures us that in the Christian Churches we are already in a "real but imperfect union." The Church's official ecumenical movement has gained real momentum since the council, and considerable progress has been made in realizing the prayer of Jesus "that they may all be one" (John 17:21). The effort in the dialogues between the various Churches has concentrated largely on closing the doctrinal gaps that have separated us. Surprisingly, we are discovering that these are not nearly as wide as we had presumed. As we talk and listen to each other in respectful dialogue, we find that on the substantive Christian message we are largely in agreement. There is happily much more that unites us than that divides us. And this bodes well for the future of Christian unification. A process is now in place that gives hope because, obviously, the Churches are steadily moving closer to each other in their march to Christian unity.

However, there is another dimension to unity which I think needs to be considered. I have often felt in my personal encounters with other Christians that there is already a shared oneness that goes beyond doctrinal convergence. It is a real oneness that is tangibly felt and experienced, however impossible it is to explain. Perhaps it is the common experience of the presence of Jesus, who assured us that "where two or three are gathered together in my name, there am I in the midst of them" (Matthew 18:20).

Thomas Merton provides a profound and helpful insight here. In notes he prepared for a talk to be delivered in Calcutta in October, 1968, he had written:

> True communication on the deepest level is more than a simple sharing of ideas, conceptual knowledge, or formulated truth. The kind of simple sharing of ideas, communication that is necessary at this level must also be "communion": beyond the level of words, a communion in authentic experience which is shared not only on a "pre-verbal" level but also on a "post-verbal" level.

Merton continues to explain that this mysterious and unexplainable communion is wordless, beyond words or speech or concept: "Not that we discover a new unity. We discover an older unity. My dear brothers [and sisters] *we are already one. But we imagine that we are not.* What we have to recover is our original unity. What we have to be is what we are."

Because, as the theologians put it, God is **"the ground of all being"** — that is, because God is the source of all that is, and especially of all human beings — we are obviously one with God from the start. We are a part of God. We are divinized people. We are not God, of course, but we are truly one with God because it is not likely that we are ever cut off from the ground and source of our being. We are clearly distinct from God but never separate from God.

Similarly, we are all of us one with one another, coming as

we do from that common source, God, who is that ground of all our being. We might even apply here the words of Jesus spoken in another context: " . . . what God has joined together, no human being must separate" (Matthew 19:6).

What Merton is rightly telling us is that at the level of doctrinal formulations we still recognize some differences, but at the level of our religious and human experience we recognize our oneness. It appears to me that the movement for Christian unity needs more and more to discover our original unity — that we are already one.

**FIRE**

# What Should We Do About Abortion?

February 2, 1990

Columnist Thomas E. Blackburn in a recent issue of the *National Catholic Reporter* suggests that pro-lifers put away their placards. He is convinced that dealing with abortion as a political-legal issue is a losing cause. I confess I have long been uneasy about the way in which the abortion debate has been conducted. We would like to expect the pro-lifers to be more judicious in the methods they use to further their cause: to protect the life of the unborn, which is admittedly sacred, God-given and most precious. Consequently, I am saddened when pro-life proponents become guilty of tactics that smack of violence in their holy war for the right to live from womb to tomb. To abort a child is clearly a violent act. It would seem to be totally counterproductive, however, for the pro-life advocates to reciprocate with a violent posture themselves while opposing the violence of the aborters. Their sometime storming of the abortion clinics obviously runs counter to both the Gospel and civil law.

I am sure that in their zeal the pro-lifers feel useful in their fight when they hold up their placards in front of the Supreme Court building on the anniversary of Roe vs. Wade. But their sometimes shrill and hate-filled voices are not likely to prove useful or productive. Blackburn is right in contending that abortion is primarily a moral issue, and moral issues are rarely, if ever, resolved at the legal-political level. Gerrymandering will not bring it to its rightful conclusion.

The Supreme Court does not cause abortions. Likewise, changing the court's mind won't stop abortions. Changing the mores of the American people will be much more difficult, but if you change the mores, you won't have to change the law. The Supreme Court's decision merely states that those who want an abortion may have one. The task of the opponents of abortion is to create a society in which nobody wants one. Once our mores oppose taking the life of the unborn, laws which forbid such taking of life will follow.

What is needed is to identify the general and particular causes of abortion. Studies will show that the reasons and causes are many and complex, but Blackburn seems to have put his finger on the underlying general cause: "Americans simply don't want to suffer," he says. They believe that suffering can be avoided by "eschewing fats, eating bran and running fifteen miles a week." If you have a headache, the television commercials promise you fast relief if you take a pain-killer; if a baby in a given situation threatens to slow you down, you can always abort it.

The American conviction that suffering is an avoidable fluke has to be challenged. It's a Gospel challenge and someone has to do it. But how? What must be conveyed is a sincere concern for the protection of life without seeming to appear judgmental, that is, without judging the woman for what she did to get into a spot where such a decision had to be made. Nor do pro-lifers strengthen their case when some high-minded males seem to be telling women what to do.

Chicago's Cardinal Joseph Bernardin offers the well-known "seamless garment" approach, which makes the right to life an across-the-board issue demanding respect for all life — from the cradle to the grave. Such a posture requires that when we sound off about abortion, we take an equally strong position against the death penalty as well as the many structural evils in our society which are life-demeaning and life-threatening. It's easier to picket the abortion clinics and the state capitols than to help a baby overcome poverty. It is incredible that some of the most vociferous pro-lifers are just as willing to send arms to Central America. By the same token, the old liberal anti-war establishment has been just as inconsistent. It never got the point about abortion. But there have been a few exceptions who, like Father Daniel Berrigan, pursue a consistent ethic by picketing against life-killing nuclear weapons as well as against abortion.

Preaching the seamless garment avoids the single-issue position which restricts its crusade to respect for life in the womb. It means preaching a whole new transformation of society where values count more than votes — a society where things and gadgets will not weigh more in the balance than persons who reflect the divine image. A society where children will not be regarded as a burden because they go to school, and schools raise taxes. Where nutritional and prenatal care programs are not the first to suffer when budgets call for cuts.

In the political arena all you can do is write a few laws that citizens in their current frame of mind will ignore. The far more difficult task will be to articulate a society with a more realistic understanding of people's problems in a highly complicated world.

Removing the particular causes of abortion is clearly going to require more skill and energy and take much more time than a series of protest marches and break-ins at the abortion clinics in trying to get a constitutional amendment prohibiting abortion. The abortion scourge will continue to haunt us until we have created a well-ordered society where no one wants an abortion and where no one sees a percentage in choosing an abortion. God speed the day when this will happen.

**FIRE**

# The Place
# for Protest in Prayer

March 2, 1990

"May I argue with God?" Henri M. Nouwen raises the question in his *Genesee Diary* and makes a good case for its allowance. He readily admits that what he calls a "spirituality of protest" was never stressed in his life. Most of us would agree that our own spiritual formation precluded any such exercise. This indicates that we are not thoroughly steeped in the Hebrew Bible, which tells us that more than a few of God's holy people engage, at least on occasion, in some pretty rough-and-tumble communication with the Lord. Abraham doesn't hesitate to haggle with the Lord about how many faithful people it will take to spare the destruction of wicked Sodom and Gomorrah. Yahweh suggests a minimum quota of fifty. Abraham, after repeated pleadings, prevails upon the Lord to reduce it to ten. After all, he argues, the quality of God's mercy is on the line.

We find Jacob of old daring to wrestle all night with God's angel rather than let him return to his heavenly abode. Jacob's conduct, hardly appropriate for an earthling in dealing with a celestial creature, suggests a boldness foreign to our experience! Ancient Job dares in the presence of the Lord to curse the day he was born because of the many afflictions which the Lord has heaped upon him.

We shudder at the angry reproach directed against the Lord in some of the psalms and find it difficult to condone this as a legitimate form of prayer. And anyone familiar with the prophets will find more than a few challenging threats hurled to the heavens in order to get the attention of a seemingly apathetic and uncaring God. Indeed, Jesus Himself, at least momentarily, seems less than totally submissive in His cry from the cross: "My God, my God, why have you forsaken me?" (Mark 15:34).

The remarkable Rabbi Abraham Heschel has this to say about the aspect of protest against God:

> The refusal to accept the harshness of God's ways in the name of his love was an authentic form of prayer. Prophets of Israel were not in the habit of consenting to God's harsh judgment and did not simply nod, saying, "Thy will be done." They often challenged him, as if to say, "Thy will be changed." They had often countered and even annulled divine decrees. . . . A man who lived by honesty could not be expected to suppress his anxiety when tormented by profound perplexity. He had to speak out audaciously. Man should never capitulate, even to the Lord.
>
> . . . There are some forms of suffering that a man must accept with love and bear in silence. There are other agonies to which he must say no.

Heschel's approach to prayer, which allows for protest against God and even for questioning God's decrees, reveals how close the Jew feels to God. This intimacy is grounded in the covenant relationship the Jew enjoys with the Lord, which is often biblically characterized as spousal — Yahweh is the Bridegroom and Israel is the beloved bride. A marriage relationship in which one could relate to God only in terms of submission would be destructive of genuine closeness, according to the Jewish approach. Jews, after all, are quite convinced that God is with them in every step of their human journey, and the lines of intimate communication with God are always open. And honest communication requires, as Heschel assures us, that we need never "suppress anxiety," and above all, "never capitulate, even to the Lord."

As Christians, we need to include in our prayer life an attitude which brings God and God's people very close to each other — so close that the dual movements of active protest and passive surrender are both present without fear of recrimination. I remain distant from God, and my relationship with God is in fact dishonest, when I am allowed to relate to God only in terms of surrender.

# When a Loved One Commits Suicide

April 7, 1990

Tim, age 26, was my grandnephew. His sudden death was all the more shattering because, in his own words, he couldn't "take it anymore, the pain is too great," and Tim died by his own hands. I addressed the following words to his grief-stricken parents, George and Mary Jo, just ten days after the Mass of Christian Burial.

Dear George and Mary Jo:
You have been very much in my thoughts these days. To the extent that I can, I want to share your pain, but I know that I cannot possibly feel what you are now experiencing in the depths of your persons. No one can quite experience the loss of a child — in your case, a very dear son — as can the ones whose flesh and blood was so generously shared in the birthing and the years of nurturing that followed. Tim was so much a

part of you that in his passing you understandably feel that a part of you has been suddenly and cruelly torn from you.

As I reflect on this, it comes to me that this boy, who was so much a part of you in life, will continue to be a part of you in your ongoing experience. The relationship that had been built up between you in all those years — yes, all those "dyings and risings" that are so much a part of every human encounter — can never be taken from you. Not only in memory, so to speak, but actually — in reality! The close and mutual bonding that your love was able to develop through the years — your loving him and his loving you — is so thick and real that it will never die. Though his physical presence has now been withdrawn, all that Tim was and is to you will never be lost.

When I think of those in my family who are already with God — my dear dad and mother, yes, and my brothers Carl and Romie — hardly a day goes by that they are not only in my thoughts, but also somehow with me still. It is difficult to articulate, but they are strangely nearer to me than just in my thoughts. And so the oneness that we share in the so-called communion of saints becomes more than an article in our creed to which we give intellectual assent. It becomes a down-to-earth experience.

I could plainly see how devastated you were last Monday at the church. Understandably so. Especially when it is sudden, death is so overpowering that it fairly numbs us. It leaves us quite beside ourselves, particularly in the early weeks when the loved one seems literally to have been snatched from us. But I was also quite impressed with the staunch faith you demonstrated. In the midst of your pain you witnessed a measure of calm and control which told me that you truly believe Saint Paul's words: " . . . all things work for good for those who love God" (Romans 8:28).

As we move into Holy Week, the example of Jesus suffering is placed before us. The prophet Isaiah in Passion Sunday's first reading refers to the Suffering Servant Song, which the liturgy applies to Jesus.

> I gave my back to those who beat me . . .
> My face I did not shield
> from buffets and spitting.
> The Lord GOD is my help.
>
> Isaiah 50:6-7

And then we come to that striking sentence which ought to ring in our ears:

> I have set my face like flint,
> knowing that I shall not be put to shame.
>
> Isaiah 50:7

I realize that in your present stage of grieving, when shock, confusion, and anger are still so much with you, it is not yet possible to "set your face like flint," in imitation of Jesus who set His face to Jerusalem to face His enemies and His suffering and death. And yet in the second reading Saint Paul reminds us that because we are Jesus' disciples, our attitude must be that of Christ who emptied Himself, obediently accepting even death (see Philippians 2:5-8).

I'm sure you know how essential it is to let your grieving time run its healing and therapeutic course. But you will also find that prayerful reflection on the Scriptures has a singular power to help you get a handle on this mystery of pain and death. Isaiah reminds us: "[My word] shall not return to me void . . ." (Isaiah 55:11). God's word can be comforting as well as challenging. Even Jesus from the cross cried out in anger and confusion when, in that terrible moment of seeming abandonment, He erupted with the words: "My God, my God, why have you forsaken me?" (Mark 15:34). These are hardly words of total acceptance. So don't be afraid to cry out in your anguish and include in your praying what spiritual writers call a prayer of protest. Like Martha in the Gospel we should feel free to complain a little: "Lord, if you had been here, my brother would not have died" (John 11:21).

Jesus' approach to our pain and suffering is significant in that He doesn't take away our suffering but joins us in our suffering. In His incarnation He identifies with our entire human situation. He sweats our blood; He dies our death. He goes all the way with us on our human journey. He becomes one with us in His redeeming love, becoming obedient "even unto death," so that in the process we can become Him, so to speak. Become, in Paul's words, Christ: " . . . yet I live, no longer I, but Christ lives in me" (Galatians 2:20).

We know that all this is still a mystery, but we need to ponder it to let a little light shine on it. To know that there is no

---

*I'm convinced that in Tim's mind the decision he made was the best he could make. . . .*

---

situation in life, no time or place, no happening in which God is not present to us, can help us. Ultimately, then, like Jesus, we will be able to exclaim, "Father, into your hands I commend my spirit" (Luke 23:46).

I'm convinced that in Tim's mind the decision he made was the best he could make — the best and the only way out for him and for all he left behind. Conceivably, it was done as an act of prudence, and from his perspective, even an act of love. Any speculation beyond this would be fruitless. And now we should leave to him that rest which he sought and for which we pray when we say: "Eternal rest grant unto him, O Lord . . ."

Nor should you in hindsight put any blame on yourself for

this happening. Parents are all too easily inclined to appropriate to themselves responsibility for any and all the actions of their children. Guilt-tripping in this instance would be most unproductive. All of us who know you, George and Mary Jo, are totally convinced that you were loving and nurturing parents throughout his life. And only you know what pain you often endured in trying to minister wisely to his many and special needs.

So peace to you! You are in the minds and prayers of all the Eschweilers as we try to share your burden.

Sincerely,

Fr. Fran

FIRE

# Death of a
# Dear Friend: Two Years Later

May 4, 1990

Just ran across the scribbled notes of my homily preached at the Mass of Christian Burial for my dear friend, Eleanore Taraboi, who died in September, 1988. I somehow feel compelled to write them down now and to shed on them that added light which comes from hindsight and further reflection. The notes were written somewhat hastily while I was still very much in the grip of shock and the throes of grief. The pieces consequently appear in a less than orderly fashion.

*   *   *

She was a feisty and earthy person — one of the most authentic persons I have been privileged to know. There was nothing of sham or pretense about her. As a consequence, she sometimes came across as blunt, even harsh. She said what she thought and thought what she said. What you saw in Eleanore was what you got — the genuine article. With her you always knew where you stood. She believed that friends should be able to level with each other because the truth is bound to make you free.

But she could also be tender — a generous person with a big heart. She had deep compassion for people. She was a benefactor of the poor of Milwaukee's inner city in ways they did not know. She spent many an hour sorting clothing and doing other jobs at Brother Booker's House of Peace on Seventeenth and Walnut Streets. It was she who originated and mothered the Good Shepherd "sister relationship" with that troubleshooting and nurturing house to which so many of God's poor in Milwaukee turn as a haven of hope. The Christmas and Easter collections of toys and cash for gift certificates were an annual outreach from the Good Shepherd parishioners to meet the basic needs of our brothers and sisters in inner-city neighborhoods. Such giving not only made us aware of their needs but also, what is more important, of our need as Christians to share what we have. It deepened our conviction that our superfluity actually belongs to the poor.

A person of deep and solid faith, she never wore her religion on her sleeve. The celebration of good Liturgy was a great passion with her. She was especially drawn to community worship where there were people and spirited music. Oh, how she loved music!

She cared little for technical theology, but she possessed an instinctive theological sense. She was a lay person ahead of her time. She understood the "people of God" theology as opposed to the hierarchical, or pyramid, church concept of pre-Vatican II. As a member of one of our first parish councils, she strove to function on the principle that the people are the Church. And as she labored with us for more than a dozen years on our Liturgy Planning Committee, she was extremely creative in constructing worship services which would help people to actively participate and pray. And she was always concerned that we keep our ears to the ground to get honest feedback from the people in the pews.

She was a firm believer in resurrected life — Jesus' and ours! "Future life's got to be better than this one," she'd say, "and

I'm going to be darn mad if it doesn't turn out to be such." The paschal mystery — dying and rising in Jesus and in us, the baptized — was the ground of her faith. She exemplified it in her life and never hesitated to preach it to me when, in my weaker moments, she found me wavering in my faith.

That was why she loved the Eucharist and was so eager to help plan our celebrations — so people could get a good grip on that mystery which had the power to transform their lives. She would often recall the words of Jesus about the grain of wheat having to fall on the ground and die before it could bring forth fruit. She seemed to understand that things often have to get worse before they can get better — that with us, as with Jesus, disintegration and death are necessary ingredients in coming to wholeness and life.

Ellie was especially skilled in working with food. She was forever setting up delicious dishes for refreshment after meetings. She was truly a Eucharist person who, like the Emmaus disciples, "had come to know him [Christ] in the breaking of bread" (Luke 24:35). For her, Christ could be found in all meals and festive eating. To her, every meal was a little Eucharist.

Eleanore was an avid and voracious reader. Never a good sleeper, she often spent long and sleepless nights in reading. Her hunger for learning enabled her to become a self-educated and an extremely well-informed person.

Above all, she had an insatiable zest for life. To her, life was a gift to be relished and used. The contagious Spirit in her could not readily be contained. The universe is the richer for her having been here, and all of us who were privileged to be friends with her will be forever in her debt. To the God who gave her to us, for all the person that she was and continues to be, for all that we are and have become because of her, our endless thanks. She loved life here. May she now and forever enjoy the harvest of life in abundance, which Jesus promised to all who believe.

# Weeds Among the Wheat

May 7, 1990

In interpreting Matthew's parable of the weeds and the wheat (Matthew 13:24-30), we can easily fall into a trap of dividing our world into good guys and bad guys. We, of course, wear the white hats, and the others wear the black hats. The parable is reminiscent, also, of Matthew's famous final judgment scene where the good guys, the sheep, are lined up on the right side of the king, and the bad guys, the goats, are rounded up (where else?) on his left. (See Matthew 25:31-46.) To want to avoid complexity and to simplify things by sorting them out in the familiar categories of good and bad is a common temptation — especially when our neat division leaves our parish, our neighborhood, and our country smugly on the side of the good.

What the parable is trying to say to us is that in the real world good and evil most often coexist — not only in society, but also in the depths of the human heart. The parable is a story of the way things are in the human condition, where things are ambiguous, where gracious deeds are intermingled with unloving ways, where you can always find a strange mix of generous responses with sudden falls from grace. Instead of black and white, we have shades of gray.

The parable teaches that in life's many choices we often

alternate between good and bad. In studying the lives of famous people, saints included, you will find (if you read a well-researched biography!) that these people are at once members of the communion of saints and the communion of sinners. While capable of heroic deeds worthy of our highest admiration, they remain vessels of clay and members of a flawed humanity. We no longer write simplistic tales about Honest Abe. The biggest lie of all, we protest, is the lie that the father of our country never told a lie. Unlike the Gospel Jesus, these heroes simply do not walk on water. When we write about human beings today, we paint them warts and all.

Like the owner's slaves in the parable, we impatiently want to pull out all the weeds at once. We want to produce a pure Church, free of sinners. But there is no such thing, for we are a pilgrim Church, not yet fully arrived. We are a mixture of sinfulness and righteousness. We try to be wheat, but sometimes we are not. We are the sons and daughters of God, made to God's image, but we know only too well that we are far from perfect. We feel somehow that the Divine Potter has made us so. Often the good seems beyond our reach and the evil, all too readily accessible. "For I do not do what I want," Paul tells us, "but I do what I hate" (Romans 7:15). It is the mystery of iniquity. We'd like to join Paul when he asks, "Who will deliver me from this . . . ?" (Romans 7:24). The owner in the parable answers simply, "Let them [weeds and wheat] grow together until harvest" (Matthew 13:30). In other words, let things be until the Lord chooses to do the final separating.

"Beware," Jesus seems to say, "of destroying that which is good in your hurry to root out the bad. Cool it — you aren't all good, you know, but you aren't all bad either. You are a blend of sin and goodness, of foolishness and wisdom. Leave it to Me. The harvest is My department. In the end you will all be judged by a Lord who is forgiving and abounding in kindness and mercy, a Lord who knows how to extract good out of what is always a strange mix of weeds and wheat."

# Priests and Laity:
# Different but Equal

June 9, 1990

In our annual priests' assembly held here a few weeks ago, one of our presenters offered a theological perspective on the priesthood. (I never tire of trying to probe what is seemingly inaccessible — the mystery of what it means to be a priest!) In our developing theology of priesthood since Vatican II, we were told, we find a profound shift in the priest's role: **from exercising sacramental power to providing ministry, or service.**

The priest today perceives himself not so much as the "magic man" or the "grace conductor" — the holy one endowed with great power over the people — but rather as one of the people of God, sharing and participating with others in the one priesthood of Christ. We are all together baptized members of the people of God, all of us called to a common mission to build up the Church. The priest is not in a niche on the wall; he does not act from above, over and against the people, but with the people. He is a fellow pilgrim, searcher, and guide. He is not one of the elite in the Church, not elevated above the laity and able to exercise over them a sacramental and mystical power.

Such was the notion of the priest developed at the Council of Trent in the sixteenth century and generally upheld until the Second Vatican Council. This was the priest who was the *Alter Christus* ("another Christ"), the man called from among the people and set apart, the "Lone Ranger" whose obedience was exclusively to the bishop and whose spirituality was better served by his withdrawing from the world and avoiding close contact with the laity. In this understanding, his sole relationship with the people took place in the celebration of the sacraments. This priest was the man with power over the Mystical Body of Christ, the Church.

Today's priest, then, is the servant of the people. He is not exclusively "another Christ" because all the baptized, all those who are christened, are other Christs with him. He indeed does possess power, properly understood. He exercises this power through **service** and **empowerment.** To be sure, from their Baptism the people are already empowered, with the power of the Holy Spirit flowing from the resurrection and Pentecost's outpouring. It is the priest's servant role to be the gatherer of the assembly (especially for the Eucharist) and to be the guarantor of the Word — that is, to proclaim the Gospel in season and out of season to the people who have a claim to that service. In all the sacraments the priest needs to break the bread of the Word. Because the sacraments are acts of faith, it is necessary that the recipients' faith be fed and enkindled in order to ensure a fruitful participation.

In this way, the priest is ever empowering the people, calling them forth to live out their Baptism and to be what they are: a priestly people endowed with special gifts. They are to be in their own right prophets, priests, and kings as they witness to Christ in the world through their worship and through their full engagement in the task of building the kingdom.

The people, in turn, empower the priest. As they are shaped by him, so, too, is the priest shaped by them. The faith of the sick whom he anoints (he shouldn't just anoint them, he should also hold their hands!), their calm acceptance of suffering and even the summons to die, the zeal of parents evangelizing their children, the creativity and enthusiasm of people at meetings and of those who prepare the music and plan the Liturgy, the response of those engaged in the work of human concerns — all these are manifestations of the gifts of the Spirit in the priestly people who, in turn, have a profound influence on the formation of the priest.

We are not talking here about two different priesthoods, differing one from the other as apples from oranges. Rather they are two different manifestations of one and the same priesthood, which belongs to Christ and to Christ alone. Each is essentially different from the other because each exists precisely for the other and is dependent on the other. Just as the priesthood of Christ made manifest in the ordained constitutes the dynamism that awakens the priesthood of Christ in the laity, so, too, the priesthood of Christ made manifest in the laity calls forth the priesthood of the ordained.

Father Peter Fink in his book, *The Priesthood of Christ,* illustrates this theology of priesthood and the differences by including these points:

(a) "The ordained minister preaches in order to awaken the summons of the word in others."

(b) When the priest presides at the Liturgy, "he prays and offers to awaken prayer and offering in others."

(c) In the priest's leadership role, "he guides and governs in order to awaken and shape in others the same pastoral care to each other that Christ shows to all."

In this way ordained ministers exercise their priesthood of the ordained in order to arouse in the baptized their own special and proper priesthood. It must be obvious that this function requires a more intense investment than what is required of those being ministered to. The demands of the one who preaches are clearly greater than those of the listeners. To lead prayer demands more than to be led in prayer, and to guide and govern more than to be guided and governed. Each then is essentially different from the other because, simply, each is dependent on the other. Different, yes, yet in a real sense also equal, sharing as we do that one priesthood of Jesus as well as common membership in the holy people of God.

I am convinced that in these fifty-five years in the priesthood I have been as much shaped by those I have ministered to as they have been shaped by my ministrations to them. We have been saving grace to each other.

# Who Do You Think You Are?

October 22, 1990

In a wonderful little book, *Song of the Bird,* Anthony de Mello, S.J., a profound mystic and compelling storyteller, spins a wonderful and insightful yarn which, to my astonishment, applies to me and perhaps to many.

A man once found an eagle's egg which he promptly put into the nest of a barnyard hen. The eaglet hatched with the brood of chicks and grew up with them. It believed that, like them, it was a chicken, and so it grew up doing what they did. It walked around the barnyard clucking and scratching the dirt for worms. Sometimes the eaglet flapped its wings and squawked, but it never learned to fly.

One day years later, after the eagle had grown very old, it saw a magnificent bird soaring high above the earth. Gliding gracefully among the strong air currents, the bird pumped its wings in easy rhythmic strokes. Awestruck, the old eagle asked, "What is that?"

"That's an eagle, greatest among all the birds," said a neighbor, "It belongs to the sky; we belong to the earth."

And so it happened — the eagle lived and died as a chicken because that's what it thought it was.

It's a sad story, really, and for many of us, it is our story. Like that eagle, we don't all reach our potential. We don't spread our wings to fly high and scan the heavens, which are our true domain. We don't get off the ground, or if we do, it is to fly but a few feet into the air. We remain stymied because we don't really know who we are. We've heard Saint Paul's words that we are "a new creation: the old things have passed away" (2 Corinthians 5:17). We've heard that we are risen people with the power of the resurrection surging in our bones, but the words have never quite penetrated into the marrow of those bones. Simply put, **we are unaware.** Perhaps that's our saving grace. Our ignorance may yet excuse us for failing to reach those heights where there are no more illusions, where we are in tune with the **really real.**

But there's more to be said. Jesus enjoins us to be wide awake and ever on the alert, to be watchful people and ever alive to what is happening. Above all, He tells us never to be afraid. He calls us to live in that awareness of the mystics who have their eyes wide open, who are so constantly focused on their true center that no matter what happens, they know "all is well" and "everything is all right." There can't be anything but good news, then, because the Spirit is with us and Jesus is Lord.

But that point of arrival will not happen without long and arduous effort, without the deep soul-searching that is not afraid to ask the right questions, which may be as crucial as finding the right answers. What are the right choices? What are the first questions that merit my full and undivided commitment?

Why is it that we who are the children of light are so often seen doing the works of darkness? The answer is simple. We have conspired to join our secular peers who have chosen to walk in the darkness, to assume a false identity which is dependent on the responses of the current milieu. Thomas Merton assures us that this secular or false self is a fabricated self that is caught up in the web of social compulsions. It is a driven self. It is not free. It is a slave to approval and ongoing affirmation. In response to the question "Who am I?" it constantly answers, "I am the one who is accepted, admired, praised, liked, hated or despised. I am the one who is in tune with the world's conventional wisdom, with the accepted norms of a secular and compulsive society."

Unlike the eagle in our story, we need to find our true self to discover who we really are. The alternative is to flounder in the murky waters of illusion. It is to live the masked life of the false self which remains earthbound, which never gets off the ground and never realizes its God-given potential to fly high. Sadly, it is to miss the wisdom encased in the words, " . . . the truth will set you free" (John 8:32).

# Judge Not

November 20, 1990

Judgment is not a human prerogative. Scripture says, " . . . judgment is God's" (Deuteronomy 1:17) and "Stop judging and you will not be judged" (Luke 6:37).

It occurred to me as I reflected this morning on Luke's account of the Zacchaeus story (Luke 19:1-10) that it is so easy to misjudge persons because what we see and observe in them is but the tip of the iceberg. There is so much beneath the surface, so much hidden in a person that escapes our observation that we invariably end up with a sad miscalculation. Luke tells us simply that Zacchaeus was a chief tax collector and a rich man. Because tax collectors were notorious for their corrupt practices, we can presume that this man, who was a "supervisor" of tax collectors in a given district, would have been engaged in corruption on a considerable scale. But as the story unfolds, there is much more to this prominent inhabitant of Jericho than meets the eye.

The townspeople, judging from the murmurings that are heard when Jesus invites Himself to dine at Zacchaeus' house that night, seem to see the tax collector exclusively as a corrupt collaborator with the Romans, and no more. But Luke's account finds that this man is far more complex than their nearsighted vision is able to detect. Zacchaeus is clearly a man who is searching for something more than what riches are able to supply. That he is looking for some kind of meaning and significance in his life is evident from his singular interest in this man from Nazareth about whom he seems to have heard so much.

There is also something amusing about Zacchaeus. He manifests a delightful ingenuity by climbing up a nearby sycamore tree to get a better view of Jesus, as the crowds pressing around him managed to obstruct his vision. (Zacchaeus, we read, was short of stature.) This would appear to be rather unseemly conduct for a man of his position in the community. But he will not be denied. And Jesus is impressed with what appears to be the beginning of a process of conversion. Seeing him there, Jesus says, "Zacchaeus, come down quickly, for today I must stay at your house" (Luke 19:5). With that Zacchaeus descends and, we are told, he receives Jesus "with joy" (Luke 19:6). The rest of the story is well known. Zacchaeus assures Jesus that he will render 50 percent of his wealth to the poor, and to all he has defrauded he will pay back fourfold.

Jesus' words — "Today has salvation come to this house" (Luke 19:9) — give evidence that there is more to Zacchaeus than his public image has led many to believe. Jesus names his true identity when He calls him "a son of Abraham" (Luke 19:9).

The Gospels are full of instances in which people are discovered to be far more than they seem when they open themselves to the saving power of Jesus. Mary of Magdala, the Samaritan woman, and the good thief on the cross are all examples that the potential for evil in all of us is matched by a capacity for goodness, especially when the divine initiative insists on taking us by the hand to forge out a new self and finally to draw us to God.

With so much still unfinished in even the worst of us, with all the potential still to be realized, with all the rich complexity that lies hidden beneath that tip which is all that we see, human judgment is obviously a futile and dangerous enterprise.

# The Gulf War and the Gospel

Winter, 1991

*The following is my response to a letter addressed to me by a suburban Catholic who took issue to a statement, "A Call for Peace," signed by me and 67 other priests from the Milwaukee Archdiocese in the early stages of the war in the Persian Gulf.*

Allow me first to introduce myself. I am a retired priest, 81 years old, ordained in 1935. I am now living at Cousins Center where I continue to be active in part-time pastoral work. Six years ago I celebrated fifty years in the priesthood.

I appreciate your writing to me and expressing your views on the "Call for Peace" statement which I signed along with some sixty-five other priests from the Milwaukee Archdiocese. I have great respect for people who reflect on public issues and take the time to put their thoughts on paper in the interest of genuine dialogue.

I do not intend to respond to all the items you noted in your letter, but simply to say some things that will put our views in perspective. As priests, we would not presume, of course, to have a "corner on the market for wanting peace," nor did we intend to give that impression. Rather, it was after deep reflection that we, as ordained ministers, felt in conscience obligated to be prophets of justice and peace at a time when the Gospel message of nonviolence and peace was hardly being voiced or heard.

When I use the term *Gospel message,* I employ it in its broad and comprehensive meaning. Jesus came precisely to "fulfill the law," as He proclaimed, to inaugurate what the Scripture scholars refer to as "the new age," the in-breaking of the kingdom of God. The constitution of this new age is stated in the radical demands of the Sermon on the Mount with its introductory listing of the Beatitudes. Such a departure from traditional precepts is in stark contrast to Old Testament requirements and conventional wisdom, which continued to tolerate and condone a practice of at least limited violence and a spirit of retaliation — which is to say a practice of "getting even."

Jesus preached and practiced nonviolence. Whenever He was a victim of violence, whether psychological or physical, He reacted nonviolently. By not striking back, He intended to **stop the flow of violence** — to stop it in its tracks, so to speak. In the end, of course, He died a violent death at the hands of enemies. Catholic teaching, obviously, does not regard Jesus' death as a defeat. He was "obedient to death"; that is, He freely accepted death for the redemption of the world. It was a redemptive death from and out of which came resurrection for Him and for us. He died for a cause, and by His nonviolent posture, He provided a powerful thrust to the development of a new age when "love your enemies," "do good to those who hate you," "turn the other cheek," "go the extra mile," "blessed are the meek," and "blessed are the peacemakers" are ideals that we as Christians are called upon at least to strive after.

I am not a strict pacifist, but I admit I am getting close to it. My view is that our modern weaponry with its powers to mass-destruct (through nuclear weapons and saturation bombing, for example) make it increasingly difficult to designate a war as just. (We somehow manage to call most wars, if not all, "just"!) You may have read or heard in the media that the religious community in the country was largely, almost universally, opposed to the Gulf War on the grounds that the means used violated the principle of **proportionality,** which is one of the points to be considered in concluding that a war is just. My view also is that this war did not come **as a last resort.** It did not appear to me that other means, especially prolonged and serious negotiations, were given sufficient time and energy to keep peace. There were mostly ultimatums and calls to "get out" on terms of what seemed to be unconditional capitulation. The invasion of Kuwait was obviously an act of blatant aggression, and Saddam's reign of terror with its incredible history of atrocities clearly needed to be resisted.

I personally wish that the President had further used his coalition-making skills and his prestige to persuade the United Nations to do in this instance what ought to be its function as a peacemaker. I do not believe that the killing of 100,000 Iraqi soldiers, and only God knows how many innocent civilians, is justified in getting rid of a brutal tyrant like Hussein. I shudder at the thought of all this destruction of life and property in a tiny country of some 17 million people inhabiting a space of about the combined size of Wisconsin and Minnesota. With our smart bombs and highly sophisticated weapons, with the great wealth and power at our disposal, we, as a nation, can hardly dare to feel proud of our achieving a quick and decisive "victory" in the Middle East. My only hope is that, in the aftermath, we will work as hard and as diligently in creating peace as we did in waging war.

Meanwhile, the present, I think, ought to be a time for grieving, rather than for self-satisfied celebrating. My heart goes out to the young men and women in the armed forces on both sides who were called upon to suffer the strains and stress of desert warfare and to engage in the horrendous task of killing their brothers and sisters in the human family. (I wince when I come across the repeated use of euphemism in the war talk. We hypocritically use terms like *losses, casualties,* and *collateral damage,* when in fact we are talking about the "D-word," which is nothing less than *death.*) My brother priests and I could hardly be accused of being unpatriotic when we opposed submitting our finest young blood to the task of perpetrating mindless destruction, and instead called for and sought the kind of lasting peace which alone can heal the wounds and brokenness of humankind.

One last thought. I was deeply saddened when the President, in his speech on Wednesday night, resorted to the triumphalism which holds that as a nation we had finally, in his words, "licked the Vietnam syndrome" once and for all. As if a war, with all its ravages on human life and Mother Earth, can ever be justified on the grounds that we need once again to feel good.

**"Let us pray for the day when war will no longer be an option."**

Sincerely,

Rev. Francis Eschweiler

# The Earth Is the Lord's

Earth Day, April 22, 1991

It is twenty years since Gaylord Nelson became the founder and father of what now commands a highly respected annual observance. Earth Day inaugurated a vision of the earth as a mother and a friend, as opposed to a garden to be exploited, plundered, and abused in the short-range interest of what we like to call economic development. The environmental movement which it spawned in this country compels us to focus once again on creation as a blessing, a gift to be shared, a treasure to be wisely used and lovingly cared for.

Earth Day reminds us that we are a people all huddled together on this great planet where, if we will have the prudence and willingness to share the rich resources lavished on us by our provident Creator, there will always be enough to go around. Yes, with no one having to go without. It is a day to remember that while the earth is our home, it is ours on lend-lease. As stewards and caretakers, we are charged with the task to build up and develop as well as conserve what the Lord of this household has chosen to hand over to us. Ours is to leave behind a permanent home for our children and our children's children.

As responsible stewards, we dare not act as though we are absolute owners of this home. The psalmist declares,

> The LORD's are the earth and its fullness;
> the world and those who dwell in it.
>
> Psalm 24:1

It is still the Lord's property and, as keepers made to the image and likeness of the primary owner, we have the task of "tending the garden" with love and respect until the day we will have to give an account of our stewardship. In the creation story narrated in the Book of Genesis, Adam (all humankind!) was told to take charge, to have dominion over this land, to perfect it and to bring it to completion. The divine Creator and Lord of the universe invites us to be participants and co-creators who will responsibly and prudently manage a planet whose resources are admittedly limited.

Prudent management requires that we do not squander this good earth's supply of air, water, and soil, of minerals, plant and animal life — all of which are intricately related to each other in a highly complex and life-sustaining ecosystem. The depletion of our precious topsoil, the pollution of our lakes and streams, the fouling of our air, with its consequent diminishing of the ozone layer, the failure to protect our wetlands and nature preserves — these are not only opposed to enlightened self-interest, but they are also a flagrant sin against the respect which God's creation so rightly deserves. Whatever we do to upset the balance and the rhythms of this marvelous ecosystem is ultimately a violent act and a sin against life. In our pro-life advocacy we are inconsistent if we fail to take measures that protect life at every step of the way. A pro-life stance must obviously include the kind of profound reverence for Mother

Earth which at once gives, nurtures and sustains the life of all that lives.

A wise man once said that we are all guests on this Planet Earth. It would of course be highly improper and rude for an invited guest at a house to upset the furniture, dirty up the bathroom and be greedy at the table. As invited guests of our gracious Host on this good earth, we can do no less than handle creation with care, accept it humbly as a gift to be received and a bounty to be shared. It is not for us to short-change those generations to come who, with us, are members of that great cosmic family. All of these are invited guests with settings in place around that grand table which is Mother Earth. As at any family table, it is only right that things get passed around.

More than all else, the earth is a temple, a holy place. It is a sacrament — the pre-eminent sign of God's presence. The stamp of the Divine is everywhere to be found here, and every last creature cries out its praise to the Lord. "The world is charged with the grandeur of God," the poet Gerard Manley Hopkins exclaims. And Daniel's canticle gets caught up in a wild and lavish exuberance in its famous litany:

> All you hosts of the Lord, bless the Lord . . .
> Sun and moon, bless the Lord . . .
> Stars of heaven, bless the Lord . . .
> All you winds . . .
> Fire and heat . . .
> Cold and chill, bless the Lord . . .
> Nights and days . . .
> Light and darkness, bless the Lord . . .
> Let the earth bless the Lord.
>
> Daniel 3:61-74

So it continues, this extravagant hymn of praise and thanksgiving to a God who will not be outdone in multiplying the wonders of creation. The refrain, "bless the Lord," is our only proper response as blessed inhabitants chosen to live here. To tamper or in any way to diminish the splendor of this earth is to desecrate a holy place. A popular song of the '60s said it well: "What a wonderful, wonderful world . . . " We have no choice but to keep it that way.

# Jesus, Liberator of Women

June 29, 1991

The word *feminism* in our day will hardly generate calm and fruitful discussion. More likely it will conjure up the usual stereotypes we tend to associate with extremists in the women's lib movement. No matter, the movement is clearly not going to go away. The issue is one whose time has come, and it is here to stay.

Like all the great liberation movements in human history — from the freeing of slaves and the establishment of constitutional and participatory governments to the continuing efforts to procure civil, religious, and political rights for all people without regard to race, color, or creed — the emancipation of women will not come without persistent and hard-nosed struggle. However euphemistically we phrase them, our notions of women as somehow inferior to men are so deeply ingrained in our culture and even in our religious heritage that nothing short of a revolution will remove the stigma, which dishonors not only woman herself but also the God whose image she assuredly bears. We will have to rid ourselves of many traditionally accepted notions that women are no more than helpmates to men, that they are the gentler but also the weaker sex, whose place is still to be restricted largely to domestic confines.

Women have admittedly made inroads into the world of the professions, the marketplace and even government, but there remains an underlying current of feeling that there is something inherently lacking in their gender makeup that will always prevent them from qualifying for the top positions in their chosen fields. Equal opportunity for women in a land that we like to proudly call a "land of opportunity" is still largely unrealized. Upward mobility in today's world is pretty much limited to male competition. There remains a feminine stereotype which holds that women lack a special competence, a certain toughness, that is needed for leadership at the top and that seems to be the exclusive prerogative of the male species.

And sadly, there remains evidence that women are still looked upon as things, as sex objects for male gratification. I have often wondered if perhaps women, as a consequence of this long-standing social perception, have not themselves come to believe that in considerable measure this is indeed their role. It is no secret that women have been known to dress, to make themselves up, and in general to conduct themselves in ways that will secure their relationships with the male population. It is unfortunate that, in so doing, women continue to allow themselves to be unfree. Could it be that Thomas Jefferson was right when he once wrote that "some people prefer to be slaves"?

My intent here is to let some of the light of the Gospel shine on this issue. Not surprisingly, the man of Galilee, Jesus, has not hesitated to rush in here in the interest of removing barriers to women's freedom. If there is one thing that is central to the message of Jesus, it is the inauguration of what He calls the reign of God, a redeemed world where no one is excluded, where all will be set free, a world in which God's embrace will be broad enough to include all men and women alike, all who bear the divine image equally. And if any preference is to be shown to any of God's children, it will be to the downtrodden, to those whom we might call the marginalized, the underclass, the underprivileged — to all those we like to lump together as "those less fortunate." Jesus had a word for these people; they were "the poor."

In His sermon on the plain, Jesus said:

> "Blessed are you who are poor,
> for the kingdom of God is yours."
>
> Luke 6:20

In His understanding, the poor were not restricted to the so-called have-nots of His day, but to all those who were powerless and who, therefore, carried a stigma — publicans, sinners, prostitutes, lepers, cripples, yes, and in considerable measure, also women and children. Jesus spoke feelingly about His Father's sun and rain falling on all people without exclusion. But His deeds also matched His words. Not only did He receive these people with open arms, He actually singled them out. He broke the established taboos of His day when He sat down and ate with them, comforted them, and, in wonderful ways, reached out to them with His healing touch. Obviously, He did not ingratiate Himself with the religious community in Jerusalem by so doing, for members of this so-called underclass were regarded as reprobate. They had been reduced to the category of the unclean precisely because they had sinned. The hand of the Lord had touched them because of their alleged infidelity.

The culture and religious tradition in which Jesus found Himself regarded women specifically as inferior to men and as second-class citizens. They had no legal rights of their own because they were perceived as being helpmates of men. They belonged to men; they were the property of men. Their role as mothers, of course, earned them a proper respect. Unfortunately, there was more than a hint here that they were sex objects, the necessary agents of procreation.

But Jesus managed to initiate a radical change in such

attitudes toward women by the way He personally treated them. He even raised the eyebrows of His disciples when He engaged in an extended theological discussion with not only a woman but a Gentile Samaritan at that — a woman who had had, by her own admission, five husbands. (It was considered unseemly for a rabbi to converse with any woman in public!) He dared to exonerate the woman who was taken in adultery. He raised to life the son of the widow of Naim because He had compassion on her. Jesus made no secret of His fondness for Mary and Martha, the sisters of His dear friend Lazarus in Bethany.

Perhaps the classic example of Jesus' willingness to break out of this mold of perceptions that demeaned women and

---

*Discrimination against women . . . clearly receives no blessing from Jesus.*

---

continued to hold them captive is found in Mark's Gospel — in that startling encounter with the woman who had suffered for twelve years with a continuing menstrual problem (Mark 5:25-34). Such a woman was regarded as ritually unclean and, because of her condition, forbidden all social contact. She was reduced to a painful and humiliating isolation. Moreover, as the Markan account indicates, she had exhausted all her financial resources in seeking medical relief to no avail. In spite of her obviously weakened physical condition, and what must have been extremely lowered morale, this woman dared to make her way through a crowd that surrounded Jesus in order to encounter Him. "If I but touch his clothes," she declared, "I shall be cured" (Mark 5:28). Immediately the feeling that she was cured of her affliction ran through her whole body, as Mark records it, and her flow of blood dried up. Jesus quickly assured her that it was her faith that cured her, and then He allowed her to go in peace.

This account says much about the sturdy faith of a truly strong woman — not one, to be sure, who could be categorized as belonging to the weaker sex. But it says even more about Jesus, whose courage enabled Him to launch with breathtaking boldness into another phase of the reign of God that He was initiating. By allowing this woman the latitude to touch Him with what was purportedly an unclean touch, and by lavishing high praise on her for the great faith which accompanied that very touch, He broke new ground in that long struggle for women's liberation which continues even to this day. Discrimination against women is still rampant in today's world, in our culture and, sadly, even in our Church; but it clearly receives no blessing from Jesus. It was for this precisely that He enfleshed Himself in our history, for which He suffered, died, and rose again. It's all contained in these groundbreaking words spoken in the synagogue:

> The Spirit of the Lord is upon me. . . .
> He has sent me to proclaim liberty to captives. . . .
>
> Luke 4:18

The word is now out. All captives — women, too — are to be set free!

# A Self-Portrait

July 22, 1989

A close acquaintance once asked me, "Just who are you, Fran Eschweiler? How would you describe yourself?" In response to that I have to be frank and say I'm not one to let it all hang out very easily. Besides, I'm not sure I'm capable of an accurate and forthright self-analysis. Having said this, I would have to say I am a complex, many-sided person. I am getting older — will be 80 years old in a few weeks. Yet in many ways I feel young at heart. I am a fairly well person, energetic, and yet not nearly as tireless as some people think. (My quick stride sometimes gives the lie to the aches in my joints.) I am a human being, living as much in the human condition as all people are. And so I suffer the normal amount of trauma, and I'm subject to the usual amount of frustration that people on this Planet Earth face.

I think I'm a person who is mostly at peace with himself, a great gift for which I am profoundly grateful. I am also a restless person with a strong urge to make a difference in the world, to use that energy and those gifts God has given me to build that kingdom of which Jesus speaks, where truth and justice and peace will prevail.

I feel that God is not yet finished with me, that more is being asked of me until I make that final crossing into the promised land of the new heaven and the new earth. For my part I am not particularly angry with anyone. I have no enemies that I can speak of. If so, I forgive them now and in turn ask their forgiveness of me. While I'm sure I am not universally loved, I try to imitate Jesus in His love for all. It saddens me to see so many unloved people in the world.

I am capable generally of being selfless and generous as well as selfish and insensitive. I have deep convictions about many things — about peace, justice, disarmament (the nuclear threat is of great concern to me!), the proper distribution and the conservation of our God-given earth's resources. I am deeply committed to bringing about reconciliation between the races. I think we need to work ceaselessly to abolish the scandal of disunity among the Christian Churches, to make the prayer of Jesus a realization in our time: "... that they may all be one ... that the world may believe ..." (John 17:21).

I am proud to be a priest, and I am especially committed to carrying out the essence of what it means to be a priest, which is to proclaim the Gospel. Celebrating a Liturgy in which the people are active participants who join their own self-giving with the total self-giving of Jesus to the Father in the unity of the Holy Spirit is at the top of my agenda. It is here at the table of the Word and the Eucharist that we declare who we are and become more of who we are as Church, a people dedicated to love and to service.

There is, of course, much more to me than I have said here. The full report of who I am will have to come from others. I think there could apply to me something of the words of the comedian Jerry Lewis, who, when Bill Janz asked him to describe himself during a *Milwaukee Sentinel* interview, said this:

> I am warm, sensitive, generous, angry, hostile, loving, selfish, selfless, and I might add, no different from anyone else suffering from the malady called human.